'TIS PITY SHE'S A WHORE • JOHN FORD

Publisher's Note

The book descriptions we ask booksellers to display prominently warn that this is an historic book with numerous typos or missing text; it is not indexed or illustrated.

The book was created using optical character recognition software. The software is 99 percent accurate if the book is in good condition. However, we do understand that even one percent can be an annoying number of typos! And sometimes all or part of a page may be missing from our copy of the book. Or the paper may be so discolored from age that it is difficult to read. We apologize and gratefully acknowledge Google's assistance.

After we re-typeset and design a book, the page numbers change so the old index and table of contents no longer work. Therefore, we often remove them; otherwise, please ignore them.

We carefully proof read any book that will sell enough copies to pay for the proof reader; unfortunately, many don't. For those we try to let customers download a free copy of the original typo-free book. Simply enter the barcode number from the back cover of the paperback in the Free Book form at www.RareBooksClub.com. You may also qualify for a free trial membership in our book club to download up to four books for free. Simply enter the barcode number from the back cover onto the membership form on our home page. The book club entitles you to select from more than a million books at no additional charge. Simply enter the title or subject onto the search form to find the books.

If you have any questions, could you please be so kind as to consult our Frequently Asked Questions page at www.RareBooksClub.com/faqs.cfm? You are also welcome to contact us there.
General Books LLC™, Memphis, USA, 2012. ISBN: 9781150325328.

❖❖ ❖❖ ❖❖ ❖❖ ❖❖ ❖❖ ❖❖ ❖❖

John Foid *m»* baptized at Ilsington in Devonshire on April 1 7, 1586. He came of a respectable family which had long lived in this neighborhood. His father, Thomas Ford, it appears from Rymer's *Fadera* (cited by Gifford) was in the commission of the peace. His mother was the sister of Lord-chief-justice Popham. " They in this county," says Fuller *(Worthies,* vol. i, p. 413, 1840), "seem innated with a genius to study law... Devonshire makes a feast of »uch who by the practice thereof have raised great estates." Ford's relationship to Popham, a man of weight and influence in the reigns of both Elizabeth and James I, may be presumed to have affected his choice of a career. For though it is probable that he matriculated at Exeter College, Oxford, in March of 1601,' we find him entered in November, 1602, at the Middle Temple, of which Popham was a member and for some time treasurer. Ford's London life, even after he became a well-recognized dramatist, re-mained closely associated with the Inns-of-Court. In Gray's Inn he had a cousin John Ford, to whom he was deeply attached, and who doubtless opened the way to a pleasant fellowship with the members of his own house. In 1629 Ford dedicated his *Lover's Mel-ancholy* "To my worthily respected friends, Nathaniel Finch, John Ford Esquires j Master Henry Blunt, Master Robert Ellice, and all the rest of the noble society of Gray's Inn." In 1633 he dedicated *Love's Sacrifice* To my truest friend, my worthiest kinsman, John Ford, of Gray's Inn, Esq. " Commendatory verses for this play were written by James Shirley, who in 1625 had taken up his residence at Gray's Inn.

Injhese days there was a powerful literary leaven in the Inns-of-Court. It is necessary only to mention the names of Bacon, Mid-dleton, Beaumont, Sir John Davies, John Marston in order to suggest some of the forces that tended to divert young men from the A John Ford

was entered under that date: see *Dictionary of National Btografhy,* article on Ford the dramatist.

leverity of their legal studies — the father of Marston, who lamented his son's seduction by the stage, had vainly bequeathed to his heir his law books in the Middle Temple. The young barrister who passed from the study of jurisprudence to the study and profession of letters was supported by many distinguished precedents. Yet for nearly a score of years after his admission to the Temple, Ford seems merely to have dallied with literary composition. So late as 1629 in the prologue to the *Lover' i Melancholy* he assumes an air of patrician superiority to those who make "the noble use of poetry a trade." Till after 1620 his work may well have been, as he is so fond of asserting that it was, the fruit of his leisure. His first literary venture, .. „ *Fame't Memorial,* 1606, is a long elegiac poem on the death of the Earl of Devonshire — a barely tolerable performance inspired by youthful enthusiasm and a desire to make himself known as a poet in polite society. Later in 1606 the visit of the King of Denmark in England gave occasion for his *Honour Triumphant or the Peers' Challenge,* a romantic treatise in prose and verse, to which was added *The Monarch? Meeting,* containing three poetical pieces in honor of the Danish sovereign. This pamphlet, like *Fame's Memorial,* was designed to commend its author to the attention of aristocratic circles. Hb next production is a lost and unpublished comedy, *An 111 Beginning has a Good End,* acted at the Cockpit in 1613. *Sir Thomat Overbury 'i Ghost,* entered in the *Stationers' Register* on the 25th of November, 1615, is also merely a name. The last performance of this period is *A Line of Life,* a moral treatise in prose, published in 1620. The moral edification of the work is insignificant; but the style shows some interesting traces of Bacon's influence, and there are some suggestive sketches of contemporaries.

After this long period of occasional, miscellaneous, and desultory writing, Ford entered upon a short period of industrious collaboration with Dekker, Rowley, Webster and perhaps others. It is a rather striking coincidence that in the year 1613, when Ford's first comedy (the lost *An Ill Beginning has a Good End*) was acted, Dekker was thrown into prison and was silent for seven years, and that Ford apparently made no further dramatic attempt till Dekker joined with him and Rowley in the composition of *The Witch of Edmonton*. This tragi-comedy was not published till 1658; but the execution _ ' of the witch referred to in the title took place in 1621; and it i generally agreed that the play was written to take immediate advantage of the interest aroused by the trial. In March, 1623-24, a moral.,„., masque, *The Sun's Darling*, was licensed for productionat the Cockpit j in 1636 it was printed with the names of Ford and Dekker on the title-page. In 1624 two other plays, *The Fairy Knight* and *Tht ' '='"' ' ' Bristoive Merchant*, were, according to Sir Henry Herbert's *Diary*, produced by the joint authorship of Ford and Dekker; but these are lost. In September of the same year a tragedy by Ford and Webster, *A Late Murthtr oj the Son upon the Mother*, was licensed for the stage, but was not published, and is now lost. Further evidence of friendly relations between Ford and Webster is to be found in the commendatory verses by the former printed in the *Duchess of Malfi*, 1623.

The production of *The Lover's Melancholy*, November 24, 1628 (published 1629), marks the beginning of Ford's independent and significant dramatic period. In the dedicatory epistle he declares.

that this is the first dramatic piece of his 'that ever courted reader," and he intimates that very likely he will not rush into print again. After a decent interval, however, he put forth in 1633 three trage-'. dies, *'Tii Pity She's a Whore*, *The Brohen Heart*, and *Love's Sacrifice*. In 16346 published his one historical play, *The Chronicle : „.-HTstory of Per-*

hin Warbech. Tht Fancies Chaste and Noble appeared in 1638, and in the following *yexifhc Lady's Trial*, the last drama to '' '" be published during the author's life-time. A tragedy, *Beauty in a Trance*, was entered in the *Stationers' Register*, September 9, 1653,„. and two comedies, beside *An Ill Beginning has a Good End*, were entered in June, 1660, namely *The London Merchant and Tie Royal " Combat;* all these were sacrificed by Warburton's cook. It remains only to add *The Queen or the Excellency of her Sex*, a tragi-comedy ' published in 1653 by Alexander Goughe, and attributed by Professor 1 „ Bang in his reprint of 1906 to John Ford.,„.,

Of Ford's later days we know nothing; after 1639 he vanishes. Gifford says there was "an indistinct tradition among his neighbour! that he married and had children." From various dedicatory epistles and complimentary verses we conclude that he lived on excellent terms with several gentlemen of the legal profession and several well-known playwrights — among the latter, Webster, Dekker, Shirley, Massinger, and Brome. He contributed verses prefixed to Barnabe Barnes's *Four Booh of Offices*, 1606; to several editions of Sir Thomas Overbury's *ff'ife;* and a highly laudatory poem on Ben Jonton to *Jonsonus Firbius*, 1638. Our knowledge of his character is mainly inferential, though his persistent emphasis upon his independence of the literary profession reveals clearly enough one of his points of pride. A line in Heywood's *Hierarchy of the Blessed Angch*, 1635,

And hee's now but *Jocke* Foord, that once was John perhaps indicates a certain loss of personal dignity which Ford suffered from his association with members of the dramatic profession. A couplet in *The Time Poets* (Choyce Drsllery, 1656) throws tome light upon his temperament:

Deep in a dump *John Fird* alone was got
With folded armes and melancholly hat.

From first to last Ford wrote to please selected judgments, «nd, though several of his plays seem to have met with tol-

erable approval, there is little evidence that he ever enjoyed wide reputation. Aside from the tributes of fellow dramatists, the most interesting contemporary mention that he received is the epigram of Richard Crashaw:

Thou cheat'st us, Ford; mak'st one seem two by art:
What is Love's Sacrifice but The Broken Heart?

Under the date March 3, 1668-69, Pepys writes in, his *Diary:* " To the Duke of York's playhouse, and there saw an old play, the first time acted these forty years, called 'The Lady's Tryall,' acted only by the young people of the house; but the house very full." In 1714 *Per/an Warbeck* was reprinted to take advantage of the excitement caused by the Jacobite insurrection in Scotland, and in 1745 't was acted on similar occasion. In 1748 Macklin revived the *Lover's Melancholy* in Drury-Lane for the benefit of his wife. ' *Tis Pity She't a Whore* was included in Dodsley's *Select Collection of Old Plays*, 1744. The beginning of Ford's modern and substantial recognition, however, is marked by Lamb's panegyric on *The Jjroken Heart* in his *Specimens ft urn the Dramatic Poets*, 1808.

gitttroUttctton

When John Ford was a young man of twenty reading law at the inns-of-court he committed two trifling literary indiscretions called *Fame's Memorialing Honour Triumphant*. These little tracts, both published in 1606, are of slight intrinsic interest, and they have passed hitherto with insignificant comment. At first sight, indeed, there seems to be no important connection between them and their author's dramatic work which began to appear in print more than a score of years later. As a matter of fact, however, they yield to closer scrutiny extremely tuggestive hints on the source of Ford's ideas and culture, on the native bias of his character, and on his peculiar conception of tragedy.

The immediate occasion of the first of these publications was the death, April 3, 1606, of the accomplished and valiant Lord Montjoy, Earl of Devonshire. Sue-cessor in Ireland to the ill-fated Essex, he had in the last years of Elizabeth's reign gained military and administrative glory. On December 26, 1605, he married Lady Rich, then divorced from her husband, and, as Giffbrd says, "by this one step, which, according to our notions and probably to his own, was calculated to repair in some measure the injury which the lady's character had sustained, ruined both her and himself.... While the Earl maintained an adulterous commerce with the lady all went smoothly; but the instant Heaven's forehead." He commends her for braving popular censure: " A beauty fairly-wise, wisely-discreet In winking mildly at the tongue of rumour." Finally he reveals the intensely romantic ground on which he stands by a veiled reference to this affair in *Honour Triumphant:* " They principally deserve love who can moderate their private affections, and level the cope of desert to the executing their ladies command, and adorn their names by martial feats of arms:... Yea, what better example than of late in our own territory? that noble, untimely-cropt spirit of honour, our English Hector Devonshire, who cared not to undergo any gust of spleen and censure for his never-sufficiently admired Opia, a perfect Penelope Penelope was the lady's given name to her ancient knight Ulysses."

The circumstances which led to the composition of *Honour Triumphant* are worthy of a brief notice. In the summer of 1606 the King of Denmark paid a visit to the English court. In honour of the occasion there were endless banquets, parades, pageants, plays, and royal joustings. Among the martial pastimes one interesting revival from bygone days of chivalry demands our attention, namely, a " Challenge of four Knights Errant of the Fortunate Islands, (Earls of Lenox, Arundel, Pembroke, and Montgomery,) to maintain four propositions relating to love and ladies, addressed to all honourable ' Men at Arms, Knights Adventurers of Hereditary Note, that for most maintenable actions wield the sword or lance, in the quest of glory.' " This entry may be found in the *Calendar of State Papers Domestic,* vol. xxn,

June i, page 319. To the notice is added in brackets, " By Wm. Drummond of Haw-thornden." It is not clear what is meant by this ascription. In 1606 Drummond was making his first visit to London, and since his father was in attendance upon the King, would naturally have been in touch with the affairs of the court. In a letter dated at Greenwich, June l, 1606 (see Drummond's *Works,* Edinburgh, 1711, pp. 231-32), Drummond gives the full text of the challenge, and names the four defenders. His wording of the four propositions, slightly different from Ford's, is as follows:

"i. That in service of ladies no knight hath free will.

" z. That it is beauty maintaineth the world in valor.

" 3. That no fair lady was ever false.

" 4. That none can be perfectly wise but lovers." Drummond adds: " The king of Denmark is expected here daily, for whose entertainment, this challenge ap-peareth to be given forth"; this does not seem to indicate Drummond's authorship. In a letter of June 28 *Works* as above, p. 233), Drummond records a humorous answer to the challenge with four counter propositions; but he remarks that "the answerers have not appeared."

The affair made the king laugh, says the Scotch poet, but the young Templar Ford was struck by the happy thought that the pen is mightier than the sword. Accordingly he brings forth his pamphlet *Honour Trium-fhant: or the Peerei' Challenge* with this motto on the title-page: *Tarn Mercuric, quam Marti—*" In honor of all faire ladies, and in defence of these foure positions following: I. Knights in ladies service have no freewill. 2. Beauty is the mainteiner of valour. 3. Faire lady was never false. 4. Perfect lovers are onely wise. Mainteined by Arguments." The four parts of the discourse are addressed to the Lords Lennox, Arundel, Pembroke, and Montgomery in the order named. The dedicatory epistle is addressed to the Countess of Pembroke and the Countess of Montgomery. There is also a saucy address "to every sundry-opin-

ioned reader" which contains the assurance that Ford is writing to please the fair and noble, and is utterly indifferent to the judgment of all others.

But what chiefly concerns us is the spirit and temper of the document itself. We should not expect much originality of thought in a youth of twenty, nor do we find it here. *Honour Triumphant* reveals a mind immersed in the chivalric romances and poetry of the Elizabethan reign, and deeply impregnated with the Platonic ideas of love and beauty best represented in the hymns of Spenser but through the medium of Italian literature widely disseminated in English. The upshot of the argument is to identify the good with the beautiful and the service of a fair lady with the pursuit of virtue. "The chiefest creation of man," says Ford, " was — next his own soul — to do homage to the excellent frame of beauty — a woman!" " To be cap-tived to beauty is to be free to virtue.'' To be excluded from the favour of beauty is a " hell insufferable." All men of valour aim at honour; but, he contends, " the The influence of Lyly's *Kupkue s* it obvious.

mark which honour directs his level to is to participate the delightful sweets of sweetest beauty." Beauty alone is a good in itself. " For men to be honoured of ladies is the scope of all felicity." This position is supported by Aristotle who says: "the temperature of the mind follows the temperature of the body." Hence it follows that if a lady is beautiful she must be good: ''as the outward shape is more singular, so the inward virtues must be more exquisite." To love a beautiful woman is the highest wisdom. Indeed, lovers are often superior to theologians in their knowledge of the divine; for theologians are occasionally distracted by human affairs; but " lovers have evermore the idea of beauty in their imaginations, and therefore hourly do adore their Maker's architecture." In conclusion: " Would any be happy, courageous, singular, or provident? let him be a lover. In that life consisteth all happiness, all courage, all glory, all wisdom."

The ardor and earnestness of Ford's

style suggest that the leading propositions of this pamphlet were to him not merely a set of pretty paradoxes, but a religion. The worship of beauty, the fatality of love, the glorification of passion — these were the fruits of an aristocratic and highly captivating mode of free thought, independent alike of public opinion, common morals, laws, and religion, and at times even clashing sharply with them. For it is clear that most startlingly unconventional conclusions may be logically derived from the fundamental principles of the religion of beauty. To take a single instance, Spenser says in his " Hymne in Honour of Beautie" that love is a celestial harmony of heart "composed of starres concent," of hearts that knew each other before they descended from their " heavenly bowres."

Then wrong it were that any other twaine
Should in love's gentle band combyned bee
But those whom heaven did at first ordaine,
And made out of one mould the more t'agree.

Suppose, for the sake of illustration, a common Elizabethan marriage, such as that of Lord and Lady Rich, in which relatives dispose of the bride for reasons of fortune and family. Subsequently the man destined by heaven for Lady Rich appears. According to the religion of beauty, it is right that they should be united; but the corrupted currents of law, morality, and church religion do not allow it.

Spenser's wish to withdraw this poem from circulation because of its dangerous implications — rinding that young readers "do rather sucke out poyson to their strong passion, then hony to their honest delight"— is a characteristic example of English ethical sense curbing the aesthetic impulse in the interest of conduct. In England this religion of beauty was then, as it has always been, an exotic; and graver heads in Ford's own time repudiated it in no mild terms, betraying their conviction that the glorification of amorous passion was a curse out of Italy, a weakness

to be condoned in youth, a vice to be condemned in maturity. " The stage," says Lord Bacon, "is more beholden to love than the life of man. For as to the stage love is ever a matter of comedies and now and then of tragedies, but in life it doth much mischief, sometimes like a siren, sometimes like a fury.... Great spirits and great business do keep out this weak passion." ' Equally striking is the judgment on love by that little known but very interesting essayist Sir William Cornwallis: "It is a pretty soft thing this same Love... the badge of eighteene, and upward, not to be disallowed; better spend thy time so then at Dice. I am content to call this Love, though I holde Love too worthy a Cement to joyne earth to earth." So far is Cornwallis from partaking in the pseudo-Platonic ideas of Ford that he is unwilling to bestow the name of love at all on the "affection" existing between the sexes, "for it gives opportunity to lust, which the pureness of Love will not endure." As further evidence of a contemporary distrust of human nature and disgust at all irregular relations, take these sentences from an excellent "Discourse of Laws" 3 which appeared in 1620: "Laws are so absolutely necessary... to make such a distinction between lawful and exorbitant desires, as unlawfull affections may not be colored with good appearances.... Whereas men be *naturally* affected and possessed with a violent heat of desires and passions and fancies, laws restrain and draw them from those actions and thoughts that would precipitate to all See his prefatory note to the edition of 1596.
Cf. Camilla to Philautus: " In Italy to lyve in love is thought no fault, for that there they are all given to lust, which maketh thee to conjecture that we in England recken love as ye chiefest vertue, which we abhorre as ye greatest vice." *Eufhues,* p. 373, London, 1900. See his essay "Of Love." *Essayes.* By Sir William Cornewallys, London, 1606: Essay 5. An essay in *lior a: Suhsecivee,* London, 1620. manner of hazards and ill, which natural inclination is prone enough to." Finally, Robert Burton after ranging widely through the

vast literature of the subject defines romantic love as a disease. "The comeliness and beauty which proceeds from woman," he says, "caus-eth *Heroical,* or Love-melancholy, is more eminent above the rest, and properly called *Love.* The part affected in men is the liver, and therefore called *Heroical,* because commonly Gallants, Noblemen, and the most generous spirits are possessed with it." ' Yet this hero-ical love, he declares, "deserves much rather to be called burning lust than by such an honourable title." It is the special passion of an idle nobility: "We may conclude, that if they be young, fortunate, rich, high-fed, and idle withal, it is almost impossible that they should live honest, not rage and precipitate themselves into those inconveniences of burning lust." 3 Now it is a significant fact that one of the few bits of contemporary evidence bearing on Ford's character tends to show that he had the reputation of a romantic amorist. In *Cboyce Drollery* (1656) there appear two lines with distinct implications:

Deep in a dump *John Ford* alone was got
With folded armes and mellancholly hat.

Ellis seems to think that this means that he was of "shy and reserved temperament." Ward glosses thus: "He *The Anatomy of Melancholy,* vol. m, p. 43, London, 1904.
' *Ibid.,* p. 57.
Ib,d., p. 69. *Choyce Drollery....* Now first reprinted from the edition of 1656. ... Ed. byJ.Woodfall Ebsworth, Boston, 1876: the reference is in a poem *On the Timt-Poeti,* pp. 5-7. is ridiculed for a tendency to self-seclusion and melancholy." But the best commentary upon the couplet is furnished by one of the curious sections of the frontispiece of Burton's *Anatomy of Melancholy.* It represents a tall, elegantly attired young gentleman standing with folded hands and wide hat pulled far down over his eyes. Beside him are books and quill pen, at his feet music and a lute, and he is labeled " Inamorato." He illustrates the section of the work called " Love Melancholy." The couplet, then, does not furnish us perhaps " that vivid touch

of portraiture" which Ellis sees in it, but it refers Ford by a conventional sign to a well recognized type. This interpretation is borne out by a passage in Cornwallis; love, he says, brings forth " songs full of passion, enough to procure crossed arms, and the Hat pulled down." ' I dwell upon this point because it goes to prove, with the other evidence, that Ford portrayed the various passions of love in his dramas from an inside view, and not with the detachment of the sovereign dramatist nor the objectivity of a scholar or a physician, but with the brooding sym- pathy of a lover.

It is especially necessary to insist upon this point, furthermore, because Ford, in spite of his fundamentally different point of view, shows a large obligation to Burton. With the single exception of *Perkin Warbeck*, he chooses for the theme of his plays some aspect of romantic or " heroical" love, and he scrutinizes the mental and physical symptoms of the lovers with something of medical interest. Like Burton, he seems to Eway 5.

believe this heroical love the peculiar affection of men and women living in luxurious idleness; for he excludes his characters from participation in field sports, war, adventure, and shuts them up where love is the only social resource — to quote Burton's own words, "in great houses, princes' courts, where they are idle *in summo gradu,* fare well, live at ease, and cannot tell otherwise how to spend their time." His characters, accordingly, being vacant of all other occupation, are completely engrossed by a single passion of love, or of jealousy, or of revenge, or of grief, which becomes sole master of their fate, and ravishes them with extravagant joy, or secretly preys upon their spirits, or hurries them swiftly down to crime and death.

In his first published play, *The Lover's Melancholy* (1629), Ford acknowledges by a marginal note his indebtedness to Burton for a passage distinguishing certain mental diseases from melancholy. It has also been pointed out that the interlude of madmen is derived from the *Anatomy.* It should be made equally clear that the germinal idea of the whole play is due to Burton. *The Lover's Melancholy* is decidedly deficient in action, but such elements of plot as it possesses seem to have been suggested by Burton's procedure in the section of his work treating of love melancholy. Ford chooses for this scene a love-sick court, and in a medico-poetical fashion studies the causes, the symptoms and the cure of love. He even introduces as an active figure among the dramatis persona; a physician who has evidently given his days and nights to the study of Burton. In this case the patients are all afflicted with love-sorrow caused by a separation from the objects of their affections. Since their affections flow in permissible channels the cure is simple; it is necessary only to re-unite the sundered lovers.

Closely related to *The Lover's Melancholy* by virtue of their common relation to the *Anatomy of Melancholy* is the play called *The Queen* (1653), recently edited by Professor Bang and most plausibly attributed by him to the authorship of Ford. Here again, with something more of plot than in *The Lover's Melancholy,* we find the same curious use of the Burtonian psychotherapeu-tics. Alphonso, the hero, is suffering from an unaccountable but intense antagonism to the entire female sex. The queen is suffering equally from a no less intense and unaccountable passion for Alphonso. Muretto, a benevolent villain who understands the nature of this heroical melancholy, deliberately goes about, like a modern practitioner of the art of mental healing, to suggest to the mind of the hero thoughts favorable to the queen. By a strenuous course of psychological treatment he restores the woman-hater to a normal condition. Hero and heroine are manipulated by the master of the show in certain typical and exciting crises of love, jealousy, and remorse to illustrate the treatment of mental aberration. The formula is apparent: Alphonso is the patient; Muretto is the physician; the queen is the cure.

The Fancies Chaste and Noble (1638) is doubtless from the dramatic, the aesthetic, or the ethical point of view one of the worst plays in the world. It admits the reader to a disgustingly indecent situation, extracts from it the full measure of repulsiveness, and then in the fifth act blandly assures as it was all an innocent hoax. The thing is bad beyond condemnation, but perhaps not beyond explanation. One may assume that it was a work of Ford's dotage. Or — and it is rather tempting— one may assume that Ford had undertaken, like his master Burton, to display not only all the common aspects of love-melancholy, but also its sinister and execrable idiosyncrasies, of which senile lasciviousness is one. *The Lady's Trial* (16 3 9), the last of the plays with happy endings, may be considered a study of groundless jealousy after marriage. The husband returning from a long journey becomes gravely suspicious of his entirely innocent wife. All the friends and acquaintances of the family rise vehemently in defense of the wife, and at length the jealous man's ill fancies are routed. The interest here lies in the delicate portrayal of the emotions of a finely fibred woman under stress of a terrible accusation, in the chivalrous feeling which her virtue excites in the breast of the least virtuous, and in the careful exposition of the various shades of feeling through which the husband passes before his confidence is restored. The play contains some of Ford's sweetest blank verse and some excellently subtle bits of characterization; but the substance of the story is altogether too slight to be stretched over a five-act drama.

If Ford had written only *The Lover's Melancholy, The Sueen, The Fancies Chaste and Noble,* and *The Lady's Trial* he would have established but small claims on the attention of posterity. Nor would *Perkin War-beck* have made him a reputation. Coming to the stage after Shakespeare, Chapman, Jonson, Dekker, Hey-wood, Middleton, Webster, Beaumont, and Fletcher, he had nothing to contribute to dramatic technique but much to learn. On the basis of the five plays so far considered one might almost be justified in rating him as an intermittently successful imitator. *The Lover's Melancholy* is a pretty thing in the Arcadian mood, but immeasurably surpassed in its kind by predecessors. As for *The Queen,* Beaumont and Fletcher had written a half dozen tragicomedies of its type as good or far better. No one who had seen *Volpone* would have endured sitting through *Tbe Fancies.* The old playgoer might fairly have regarded *The Lady's Trial* as a tame, uneventful, somewhat modernized version of *The If inter's Tale. Per kin War beck* is a carefully constructed, well written, and highly respectable specimen of the English historical play. Produced at a date long after the vogue of the chronicle play had died away, it has attracted attention by its solitariness and has been highly praised. Placed beside *Edward 11, Ricbard 111, Henry IV* or *Henry V* it looks distinctly anaemic. Our dramatist, on the strength of this evidence, seems to lack ideas. He catches a glimpse of an interesting dramatic situation, but he lacks the imagination to follow out its evolution.

Many situations in the two plays are parallel, and the supposed character of Octavio has something in common with that of Volpone. The amount of credit that Ford should receive for *The Sun't Darling* and *The Witch of Edmonton* is still disputable and, like most problems in collaboration, probably always will be. Since space does not permit of any profitable discussion of them here, I prefer to pass them with a reference to F. F. Pierce's two articles on the collaboration of Dekker and Ford in *Anglia,* xxxvi (1912).

He has a certain penetrating insight into the passionate moods of the spirit, but he lacks the power of inventing characteristic action for the display of those moods. Frequently he sets to work in a very mechanical fashion to contrive a story to fit his characters, and, being a feeble plotter, too often contents himself with presenting the persons of the main plot in a flimsy patchwork of scenes pieced out to the length of a play by an irrelevant and tedious sub-plot. By common consent it has been decided that wit and humour were omitted from his en-. dowment, and that his comic characters are among the worst in the history of the English drama.

Upon what, then, does Ford's reputation rest? Indubitably upon his three tragedies, *'Tis Pity, The Broken Heart,* and *Love's Sacrifice,* all published in 1633. Like many another man of distinct but strictly lim-,' ited genius, Ford had two or three original ideas in him,, ' uttered them with power, and then in a vain effort to repeat his success puttered on from bad to worse. The fact seems to be that his genius remained somewhat lethargic unless his heart was engaged. It is highly significant that in these three really noteworthy plays his theme is forbidden love. In each case he confronts what he regards as an essentially tragic problem; and his constructive power, his characterization, and his poetry rise to the occasion. In each case _he approaches his material with certain romantic preconceptions which give to his treatment of illicit passion an impressive consistency. He appears to believe still, as in his youth, that love between the sexes is of mystical and divine origin, that it is irresistible, and that it is the highest good, the end and aim of being. This certainly is the creed of his tragic characters. They believe in it uncompromisingly; for it they are ready to die, reiterating their faith in the last disgrace and agony. In discussing the peculiar tragic effects which issue from this romantic creed I shall disregard the conjectural dates of the plays, and take them up in a kind of climactic order. This procedure is warranted by the facts, first, that the dates of composition appear to be indeterminable, and, second, that the dates of composition do not affect the present discussion.

The Broken Heart presents a clearly defined moral problem. Penthea, very much in love with Orgilus and betrothed to him, is forced to marry Bassanes. Orgilus, taking a purely rationalistic or idealistic view of the matter, refuses to acknowledge any validity in the union of Penthea and Bassanes. Frantic with indignant passion he cries:

I would possess my wife; the equity
Of very reason bids me.

Penthea with a supreme effort preserves self-control, and urges her desperate lover to resign himself to the irrevocable, pleading that the true quality of their mutual affection will best show itself in virtuous submission to necessity. Which of the two is right? In Elizabethan times when parents disposed of their children in a rather more highhanded fashion than now obtains — when Penelope Devereux was carried protesting to the altar to marry Lord Rich — was it not a fair question?

By a subtlety in feminine characterization unsurpassed ! if not unequalled in the period Ford reveals the full tragic meaning of the problem. Penthea's conduct in this difficult crisis is beyond criticism. She shows tenderness to her lover without tempting his weakness. She admits that they have been grievously wronged, but she will not consent to his righting that wrong by another. Under the burden of her own sorrow she finds strength to comfort his. Yet she is intensely human even at the height of an almost saintly renunciation; though she has the rare charity to wish him happy with another wife, she feels a sensitive solicitude for that wife's opinion of her. When she has finally been forced to send her lover away with sharp words, she is torn by the conflict of love and honor, and is dissolved in pity for the suffering of the unhappy man. Having resolved, come what may, to respect the ceremonial bond, she must fight for honor in a long and silent inner struggle in which victory is attended with no less misery than defeat. For she is held in a living death by her relations with Bassanes, her husband. The situation has been a favorite on the modern stage. She is impaled on the horns of a dilemma —dishonor in the arms of Or-gilus, dishonor in the arms of Bassanes. Because she is a woman and the weight of convention is heavy upon her, she chooses the legitimatized rather than the unle-gitimatized shame. Yet at last her revolted spirit bursts into speech; and she begs her brother Ithocles, who was instrumental in her marriage, to kill her. " How does thy lord esteem thee? " asks the now remorseful brother. Penthea's reply approaches the unbearable:

Such an one

As only you have made me; a faith breaker,
A spotted whore; forgive me, I am one,
In act, not in desires, the gods must witness.

For she that's wife to Orgilus, and lives

In known adultery with Bassanes

Is at the best a whore. Wilt kill me now?

This tremendous sense of involuntary pollution in a woman legally blameless and in the vulgar sense perfectly respectable is a new note in the drama and an important one.

Penthea's high-strung soul cannot for long endure the strain. Her mind begins to break down under the omnipresent horror of her unclassified sin. Stroke by stroke Ford makes it appear more and more dubious whether she has chosen the better part. With wits wandering on the verge of final dissolution she turns in the last gasp of her strangled emotion to the well-beloved Orgilus, murmuring of bride's laces and gathered roses. Over all still broods the undying horror; from the depths of pure pathos, from the ultimate bitterness of a ruined life comes her cry:

Since I was first a wife, I might have been

Mother to many pretty smiling babes;
They would have smiled when I smiled, and for certain

I should have cried when they cried; truly, brother,

My father would have picked me out a husband,

And then my little ones had been no bastards;

But 'tis too late for me to marry now,
I am past child-bearing.

Such a revelation of complex tragic emotion in the soul of a pure woman cannot be found elsewhere in the old drama, even in Shakespeare — perhaps I should say, least of all in Shakespeare. I wish here to accent the words "complex" and "pure." Desdetnona, for example, is pure; but her tragic emotion is simple. The tragic emotion of Cleopatra, on the other hand, may be described as complex; but she cannot be described as pure. And in general the tragic heroines of the period range themselves under one banner or the other: under Desdemona's, Aspatia in the *Maid's Tragedy,* the Duchess of Malfi, and Dorothea in the *Virgin Martyr;* under Cleopatra's, Tamyra in *Sassy D' Ambois,* Evadne in the *Maid's Tragedy,* Vittoria in the *If bite Devil,* and Beatrice-Joanna in the *Changeling.* There is perhaps a third class of those who, like Mrs. Frankford in the *Woman Killed with Kindness,* are neither pure nor emotionally complex — weak sisters who are perfectly conventional even in their sins. The orthodox and un-adventurous ethics of the majority of the Elizabethan dramatists are seen in nothing more distinctly than in the fact that they keep their pure women out of moral dilemmas. In their representation of life the world may break the hearts of the innocent, but only the wicked, it seems, may break their own hearts. The tragic emotions of the pure are simple, because their disaster comes upon them from without; the tragic emotions of the guilty are complex, because their disaster is due to a discord in their own souls. In *The Broken Heart* Ford throws down the gauntlet to orthodox morality by placing a thoroughly pure woman in a genuine moral dilemma. This is his most notable innovation. By establishing the tragic conflict of Penthea in her own spirit, he makes of her a distinctly modern type of heroine. In a mood of high and poignant seriousness he shows that keeping the laws and statutes may sometimes make against virtue, and the preservation of honor be the wreck of peace.

Before leaving this play we must give a word to the eminently Fordian but far less complex character of Orgilus. Convinced that Penthea's resolution will never be moved, he fixes all his thoughts on revenge, and, in a kind of icy ardor or madness, murders Ithocles; for which he is sentenced to death with the approval of those surviving in the last act. It is to be noted, however, that he welcomes death, dies bravely, and absolutely unrepentant. The man is really depicted as a martyr to the strength and fidelity of his passion; he is an un-compromising idealist. The laws against murder must be recognized; but by emphasizing the outrage which Orgilus has suffered, the vehemence of passion by which he is consumed, and the stoical calm with which he meets his fate, Ford has made him appear rather a victim than a monster. The death of Penthea, the murder of Ithocles, the execution of Bassanes, and the death of Calantha all prove how fatal it is to offer resistance to omnipotent love.

Love's Sacrifice, which treats of a more advanced degree of forbidden love than *The Broken Heart,* arouses in the reader a mingled feeling of admiration and disgust. It is not so evenly and carefully composed as *The Broken Heart.* It admits unenlivening comic scenes and an extensive and repulsive sub-plot. It employs prose freely, whereas *The Broken Heart* is entirely in verse. Finally its moral issues are very badly defined, and it ends weakly in dense moral confusion. On the other hand, the plot of *Love's Sacrifice* is a more modern conception. The principal characters are drawn with a bolder and more energetic stroke. The atmosphere has a warmth and color not found in the Spartan play. And in the two or three best scenes there is a sheer dramatic intensity unsurpassed elsewhere in Ford's work. *Lofc's Sacrifice* is distinctly modern in conception, for it deals seriously with "elective affinities" after marriage. The Duke of Caraffa loves and marries Bi-anca, a respectable woman of inferior rank, who respects her husband's position and virtues but feels no great affection for him. Then appears Fernando, young, handsome, captivating, the third person of what we have learned to call the " inevitable triangle." He conceives a violent passion for Bianca, which, as often as he declares, she virtuously repulses. But these oft-repeated protestations of love, though they do not at once conquer her will, insidiously take possession of her heart. The critical turn in the unequal duel is subtly conceived. In a moment of unusual temptation Fernando renews his fiery pleading, and once more Bianca with greater vehemence and asperity than ever spurns him from her. The impetuous lover is at last touched in his better self by her constancy, and begs forgiveness; which being granted, they bid each other good-night. But alas for the perverse reactions of the human spirit! Bianca's virtue has cooled Fernando's passion; but Bianca's passion is kindled by Fernando's virtue. While he assailed her, she stood on her guard; when he desists from his attack, her defenses fall. Distraught with stifled emotions, she steals into Fernando's chamber, clad only in her night mantle, and finds him sleeping. His quick forgetfulness bewilders her. She wakes him, and, as if frenzied by some demoniac power, lays bare her soul in an agony of confession, in shame and in sorrow:

Howe'er my tongue
Did often chide thy love, each word thou spak'tt
Was music to my ear; was never poor,
Poor wretched woman liv'd that lov'd like me,
So truly, 10 unfeignedly.
I vow'd a vow to live a constant wife:
I have done so; nor was there in the world
A man created could have broke that truth
For all the glories of the earth but thou,
But thou, Fernando! Do I love thee now?

Fernando, amazed by her abandonment to a passion to much more imperious than his own, can only gasp,
" Beyond imagination! " She hurries breathlessly on:

True, I do,
Beyond imagination: if no pledge
Of love can instance what I speak is true
But loss of my best joys, here, here, Fernando,
Be satisfied, and ruin me.

Again Fernando is so stunned that she has to make veiy clear what she means. But on the heels of surrender she cries:

Mark me now,
If thou dost spoil me of this robe of shame,
By my best comforts, here I vow again,
To thee, to heaven, to the world, to time,
Ere yet the morning shall new-christen

day,
I'll kill myself!

Say what we will of the character of this woman — and there is little question what we shall have to say — here is the very whirlwind of conflicting emotions. It is doubtless a situation which should never be shown upon the stage; but it is wonderfully realized. It is morbid; but it is terrific — this love which must express its uttermost, though the cost be death. Beside the tragic tempest in the body and soul of the woman, Fernando's ardor seems but a little warmth of the blood. He shrinks before the storm he has raised, and, scarcely more from consideration than from terror, he refuses her sacrifice. The momentous meeting ends with mutual vows of love which is to keep on the hither side of criminal realization.

Up to this point the main story is conducted with great strength and skill. The characters are clearly conceived and consistently portrayed. The action is clean and swift, with telling interplay of opposed wills strained in the crisis to the breaking point on the brink of disastrous decision. But after the supremely dramatic midnight meeting Bianca and Fernando begin to lose their bearings, and unhappily Ford seems to lose his bearings, too. The lovers grow less and less Platonic; their pledges prove poor shifts with the devil. In the fifth act they are indulging in dangerous speculations. Bianca speaks:

Why shouldst thou not be mine? Why should the laws,
The iron laws of ceremony, bar
Mutual embraces? What's a vow? a vow?
Can there be sin in unity?
I had rather change my life
With any waiting-woman in the land
To purchase one night's rest with thee, Fernando,
Than be CarafFa's spouse a thousand years.

The duke interrupts their embraces with drawn sword. Instead of showing fear or imploring pardon, Bianca turns hussy, flaunts her love for Fernando, and courts death, although at the same time she declares that she is innocent.

Goaded at length to fury, the duke gives her a mortal wound. Bianca dies with these extraordinary words on her lips:

Live to repent too late. Commend my love
To thy true friend, my love to him that owes it;
My tragedy to thee; my heart to — to — Fernando.

And so the tragic heroine passes away without a thought of repentance, without a shadow of suspicion that she has anything of which to repent. Indeed she accepts her martyrdom, confident of her innocence as a very Desdemona. Her great love for Fernando she wears as a crown of glory. Yet, it is sufficiently plain, though she has abstained from the sin of the flesh, that her mind is as spotted with adultery as the merest strumpet's.

Moreover, from this scene to the end of the play it is indubitable that Ford takes precisely Bianca's position — that he wishes to leave the impression that she is a perfectly irreproachable woman. He makes Fernando assure the duke's counsellors that "a better woman never blessed the earth." They agree, and take his side against the "jealous madman," her husband. At the point of death Fernando assures the duke that the world's wealth could not redeem the loss of " such a spotless wife." The duke agrees, and repents of his "hellish rage," declaring that "so chaste, so dear a wife" no man ever enjoyed. His faithful secretary, who first awakened his suspicions, is to be hanged on the prison top as a damned villain till he starve to death. He looks upon himself— so do the rest — as a rash murderer. In remorse he commits suicide, having first given orders that he be buried in one tomb with his chaste wife and his " unequalled friend," Fernando! And in his last breath he hopes that his fate will be a warning to jealous husbands.

Now the conclusion of this play must seem to every person of normal sense singularly wrong, weak, and futile. In the beginning of it every one knows what is decent; in the middle Fernando and Bianca grow skeptical as to what is decent; in the end no one knows what is decent — not even the author. That is the impression *Love's Sacrifice* makes upon the modern reader. Nevertheless, Ford would doubtless have denied that there had been any moral vacillation on his part; and, indeed, it is not difficult to show that he has treated his theme in perfect consistency with his romantic convictions. Love, as he had declared in *Honour Triumpbant,* he regarded as the supreme good in life and as the irresistible master of the destinies of those whom it has joined together. Bianca and Fernando, therefore, in loving each other even unto death are not only fulfilling their inevitable destinies, but are also pursuing their supreme good. Of course, Ford might say, it was unfortunate that they did not meet before Bianca was married. That was their fatal misfortune; that was their tragedy. Yet on the whole how nobly they conducted themselves under the stress of adverse circumstances. They recognized the general force of the matrimonial bond, and they withheld from their love its natural sustenance in order not to violate that bond. As for refraining from love itself, that were as impossible as drawing the stars from their courses. Even the jealous husband, then, must confess that they conformed to the limit of their power with the conventions of this somewhat helter skelter world. In some such fashion as this Ford himself must have justified the work.

' *Tis Pity* is extremely interesting both as a play and as a psychological document; for it represents the height of Ford's achievement as a dramatist and the depth of his corruption as an apostle of passion. The utterances of critics upon it from the seventeenth century to the present day emphasize the necessity of a divided judgment. Langbaine declared "that it equals any of our author's plays; and were to be commended, did not the author paint the incestuous love between Giovanni and his sister Annabella in too beautiful colours. " Lamb pointed out that "even in the poor perverted reason of Giovanni and Annabella, we discover traces of that fiery particle, which in the irregular starting from out of the road of beaten

action, discovers something of a right line even in obliquity, and shows hints of an improvable greatness in the lowest descents and degradations of our nature. " Gifford substantially reiterated the sentiments of Langbaine: "It the poetry is in truth too seductive for the subject, and flings a soft and soothing light over what in its natural state would glare with salutary and repulsive horror." Fleay is even more biting; he says: "Well allowed of, when acted, by the Earl of Peterborough to whom he dedicated it. So it is now by some critics and publishers... but not by any well regulated mind." In connection with Fleay's, the comment of Ellis is striking: "In *'Tis Pity,"* says Ellis, '' Ford touched the highest point that he ever reached. He never succeeded in presenting an image so simple, passionate, and complete, so free comparatively from mixture of weak or base elements as that of the boy and girl lovers who were brother and sister. The tragic story is unrolled from first to last with fine truth and clear perceptions." Ward says, "The poison of this poetic treatment of mortal sin is dissolved in a cup of sweetness.'' Schelling finds in it " consummate poetic art... a strange and unnatural originality like a gorgeous and scented but poisonous exotic of the jungle."

Of all these criticisms Lamb's seems to me the most penetrating and the most illuminating. Speaking in his poetical Brunonian fashion of " that fiery particle " and the "something of a right line even in obliquity" he touches upon the intense romantic idealism which marks all Ford's lovers, and which is the fundamental and controlling spirit in all Ford's most characteristic work. It will not do to attribute his amazing attempt to excite sympathy for the depraved hero and heroine to the general spirit of the time; the unnatural passion which is the theme of his play was quite as abhorrent to common feelings in the age of Charles I. as it is today. Indeed, there is some evidence that it was even more abhorrent. In the *Calendar of State Papers for 1631,* two years before the publication of ' *Tis Pity,* is recorded under the date of May 12 a "sentence of

the ecclesiastical commissioners upon Sir Giles Allington for intermarrying with Dorothy Dalton, daughter of Michael Dalton and his wife, which latter was half-sister to Sir Giles." A few days later the Rev. Joseph Mead writing to Sir Martin Stuteville dwells upon the im-pressiveness of the trial at which eight bishops presided, and upon the heavy penalties imposed, which included a fine of £2000 upon the procurer of the license. In conclusion Mead writes: " It was the solemnest, the gravest and the severest censure that ever, they say, was made in that court."

It is possible that this case, doubtless the talk of London, may have suggested to Ford the composition of *'Tis Pity.* It was exactly the situation to appeal to hi« sympathies as a poet and to his interest as a lawyer. Here again, as in the Devonshire-Rich affair, the impulses of the heart were in conflict with the world's laws as defined by the ecclesiastical court. The Bishop of London had pronounced Sir Giles Allington's marriage a most heinous crime. But Ford did not look to bishops for his moral judgments; his court of last appeal was the small circle of those unfettered spirits who recognized a kind of higher morality in obedience to the heart. It would at any rate have accorded with his temper and his previous work to write a play presenting a case of incest much more flagrant than that before the *Court and Times of Charles l.,* vol. n, p. n9.

public yet so veiled with poetical glamour as to elicit for the criminals both pity and admiration. That, at least, is what he did.

He approaches the theme not with the temper of a ttern realist bent on laying bare the secret links of cause and effect in a ferocious and ugly story of almost unmentionable lust and crime, but with the temper of a decadent romanticist bent on showing the enthralling power of physical beauty and the transfiguring power of passion. He accordingly makes the ill-starred Giovanni and Annabella the well-bred offspring of a prosperous gentleman of Parma. The young man has had every opportunity of religious training, study at the university, and intercourse with good society. The girl, brought up carefully in her father's house, is endowed with every grace of mind and body, and is flattered by the attention of distinguished suitors.

But like their author they have been nourished on that great mass of Renaissance literature which in Italy and in England establishes the religion and theology of earthly love. In the opening scene Giovanni, already in the throes of passion, fortifies himself with philosophical authority, casuistical argument, and Platonic nonsense quite in the vein of Spenser's hymns. Shocking as it is, we must recognize that this blossomed corruption is rooted in the fair garden of Elizabethan romance. To Giovanni, as to the youthful Spenser, love is the supreme thing in the world, beauty the unquestioned object of adoration. Since he finds this adorable beauty in his sister, his soul conforming to its celestial nature must bow and worship. Duty in its ordinary sense is not in this field at all; the soul's duty is complete submission to the divinity of beauty —

Must I not praise
That beauty which, if fram'd anew, the goda
Would make a god of, if they had it there,
And kneel to it, as I do kneel to them?

This note is struck again and again; thus in complaint:

The love of thee, my sister, and the view
Of thy immortal beauty have untun'd
All harmony both of my rest and life.

Thus argumentatively:

Wise nature first in your creation meant
To make you mine, else't had been sin and foul
To share one beauty to a double soul.

In another more extended passage he actually makes the Platonic identification of the good and the beautiful, repeating in part exactly the argument which Ford had employed in *Honour Triumphant* when defending the position, " Fair lady was never false ":

What I have done I'll prove both fit and good.

It is a principle which you have taught,
When I was yet your scholar, that the frame
And composition of the mind doth follow
The frame and composition of the body:
So where the body's furniture is beauty,
The mind's must needs be virtue; which allow'd,
Virtue itself is reason but refin'd,
And love the quintessence of that: this proves,
My sister's beauty being rarely fair
Is rarely virtuous; chiefly in her love,
And chiefly in that love, her love to me.

According to the romantic creed the worship of beauty is not merely the soul's duty; it is also thesoul' necessity. Hence Giovanni's reiterated accent upon fate:

Lost! I am lost! my fates have doom'd my death:
The more I strive I love.

Giovanni distinguishes between the common motions of the blood and the inexorable power not himself:

Or I must speak or burst. 'Tis not, I know,
My lust, but 'tis my fate that leads me on

He recognizes that resistance to this power is mortal:

'Tis my destiny
That you must either love, or 1 must die.

Under the stress of his passion Giovanni becomes an absolutely uncompromising exponent of Ford's romantic idealism. In the first part of the play he exhibits some regard, though slight respect, for ordinary morality. But he is soon brushing aside his scruples with the impatient inquiry:

Shall a peevish sound,
A customary form, from man to man,
Of brother and of sister, be a bar
"Twixt my perpetual happiness and me?

And before long he has resolved that prayer and heaven and sin are " dreams and old men's tales to fright unsteady youth." In this conviction he is confirmed by Annabella's acknowledgment

that he had captivated her heart long before he challenged her to surrender. By making her yield at once with an abandon equal to Giovanni's Ford plainly intends to show that the souls of the brother and sister were predestined for union in that Platonic heaven of lovers whence they came. With this conviction strong upon them both, they fall upon their knees and vow the most astounding vow by the sacredness of their mother's ashes to be true one to the other. It is the passionate fidelity of Giovanni to his vow, his desperate single-mindedness, which lends to this terrible transaction its evil splendor. Later, under the shadow of impending doom, the Friar makes a vain effort to shake the young man's resolution. If it were possible for a moment to forget the monstrosity of the affair, the fierce ecstasy of Giovanni's reply might stir a tragic thrill: *Friar.* The throne of mercy is above your trespass; Yet time is left you both — *Gio.* To embrace each other,

Else let all time be struck quite out of number.

So, too, the martyr-like rapture of Annabella when, her crime confessed, she is threatened by her husband with instant death: *Che morte piii dolce cfie morire per amore f* and as he hales her up and down by the hair: *Morendo in graxia dee morire senza dolore.*

As the fatal net closes around the lovers, Ford seems to summon all his powers to represent their misery as the price of their devotion to the highest ends of which their souls are capable. Giovanni nerves himself to take vengeance upon his enemies that when he falls he may die a "glorious death." He slays his sister—not in a blind rage, but to save her from the vile world — tenderly and with a kiss and crying:

Go thou, white in thy soul, to fill a throne
Of innocence and sanctity in heaven.

Then turning away as from the sacrifice of a white lamb without blemish to the god of love, this fervid idealist, fresh from adultery, incest and murder, bids his heart stand up and act its " last and greatest part " — another murder! Dying, he seals with his last breath his faith in the passion that has wrecked his life:

Where'er I go, let me enjoy this grace,
Freely to view my Annabel's face.

Now it appears to me incontestable that a dramatist who seeks such effects as ' Tis Pity produces must write with a conscious and clearly-defined theory. Ford cannot be explained as an imitator of his contemporaries; for his impressive attempt to make his auditors believe in the whitenesss of a soul despite the abhorrent pollution of its fleshly envelope is without precedent in the English drama of his age.' The man is original in his fundamental conception of the nature of tragedy. I am not sure, with Havelock Ellis, that Ford "foreboded new ways of expression "; his analytic power, so much commented upon by his critics, he shares with Shakespeare and Middleton and Webster. I think it clear, however, that, so far as English drama is concerned, he did forebode a modern conception of the tragic conflict. That is to say, while his contemporaries continued to represent the tragic catastrophe as the disastrous issue of a clash between good and evil, he seized the subtler and more bitter and less salutary notion, familiar enough to-day, that the tragic catastrophe results from the clash of the relative good with the absolute good. In other words, he foreboded a new way of envisaging morality. Recall Giovanni's valediction to the soul of his sister, and then read these words from Maurice Maeterlinck's ' Treasure of the Humble: There is sufficient nondramatic precedent; compare these lines from Spenser's " Hymne in Honour of Beautie":

Nathelesse the souk is faire and beauteous still,
How ever fleshes fault it filthy make;
For things immortal no corruption take.
" It would seem as though our code of morality were changing, advancing with timid steps toward loftier regions that cannot be seen. And the moment has perhaps come when certain new questions should be asked.... What would happen if the soul were brought into a tribunal of souls? Of what would she be ashamed? Which are the things she fain

would hide? Would she, like a bashful maiden, cloak beneath her long hair the numberless sins of the flesh? She knows not of them, and those sins have never come near her. They were committed a thousand miles from her throne; and the soul even of the prostitute would pass unsuspectingly through the crowd, with the transparent smile of the child in her eyes.' ' It is noteworthy in this connection that Maeterlinck has adapted 'Tis Pity for the modern stage: see Bibliography. M. Maeterlinck is, of course, also familiar with Platonic and Neo-Platonic theories. His modern heresy is simply a resuscitation of an obsolete, poetical commonplace.

Charles Lamb rather curiously quoted as comment upon his selection from this play a sonorous passage of Sir Thomas Browne's Pseu-dodoxia Epidemica, of which this is the gist: " Of sins heteroclital, and such as want either name or precedent, there is oft-times a sin even in their histories.'' Weber, Gifford, and Dyce in their complete editions of the tragedy have with even less appositeness reproduced the passage. Loath to depart from the fine tradition — now a century old — of remembering Browne on this occasion, I respectfully suggest to future editors of Ford the substitution of the following maxims from Christian Morah: " Live by old ethics and the classical rules of honesty. Put no new names or notions upon authentic virtues and vices. Think not that morality is ambulatory; that vices in one age are not vices in anotherj or that virtues, which are under the everlasting seal of right reason, may be stamped by opinion. And therefore though vicious times invert the opinions of things, and let up a new ethics against virtue, yet hold thou unto old morality."

Whatever we may think of Maeterlinck's mystical theory — I, for one, consider it beautiful and pernicious nonsense — it is worth while to observe that his dramatic illustration of it is entirely different from Ford's. He has the tact to perceive that plays built upon this theory have no place upon the realistic stage. He is even doubtful whether genuine tragedies of the spirit can be fitly

represented by actors at all. They must touch the sympathy of the reader invisibly as he sits brooding in quietness, and like the indefinable appeal of music be felt rather than understood. Accordingly in his earlier work Maeterlinck divested his scene of every reminder of the gross and to him insignificant physical world, in order to make clear a stage for the interaction of almost disembodied spirits. In the dim light of the wan Arthurian realm where his tragedies are set, the passions ebb and flow with the tides of an unplumbed and uncharted sea, by whose waters naked soul meets naked soul under the wings of destiny. No question rises there of heredity, training, environment; for only immortal and immaterial essences are there engaged; and they cannot be affected by these mortal and material forces.

Ford's theory of the inviolability of the soul has much in common with Maeterlinck's. It seems, however, much more startling because it is clothed in very human flesh and blood, and set upon a realistic stage. Ford presents his hero and heroine, for such they must be called, in the light of common day. He prepares us for a tragedy in which we should witness the operation of the laws of this world; but he presents us a tragedy in which the protagonists are emancipated from the laws of this world, and act in accordance with the laws of a Platonized Arcadia. They are idealists in one world, but criminal degenerates in the other.

The originality of 'Tis Pity has been pretty generally conceded, at least by English critics; but it hai not always been made sufficiently clear that the originality lies in the treatment and not in the choice of the theme. As a matter of fact this subject was handled by several of Ford's important contemporaries, and it may be worth while briefly to indicate their decisively different method of approaching it. The crime here involved constitutes, it will be recalled, one of the iniquitous elements in the marriage of Claudius and Gertrude in Hamlet, and it furnishes a shuddering background of horror for the first act of Pericles. To the healthy mind of Shakespeare it is clearly a matter abhorrent. It is m part of a tangled web of lust which Tourneur made into the *Revenger'i Tragedy.* But though Tourneur chose corrupt material, he dealt with it in a sound fashion. With him there was no poetical glazing, no veil of illusion cloaking the beast, no scape-goat fate occupying the place of the abdicating will, no " higher morality" subtly aspersing common decency. When his characters commit gross or unnatural crimes, he makes it perfectly apparent that the moving force is bestial drunkenness or physical degeneracy, not celestial foreordina-tion. Thus the incestuous Spurio cries:

I was begot in impudent wine and lult.

Step-mother, I consent to thy desires.

Beaumont and Fletcher's *King and No King* has for its central theme the love of Arbaces for his supposed sister, Panthea. But in the end it transpires that Arbaces is a changeling, and in reality not related at all to Panthea. Nevertheless the authors do not wholly rely upon the unexpected denouement to explain the moral aberration of the hero. They tell us in the first place that Panthea was but nine years old when Arbaces left her not to return till she had reached her maturity; consequently he appears to be smitten rather with a fair stranger than with a sister. And in the second place they spare no pains to present him as a man of abnormally violent and unruly temperament. Furthermore, when after fearful struggles his passion begins to master him, he does not justify himself as an apostle of love and beauty and their "higher" reasonableness; on the contrary he declares:

I have lost

The only difference betwixt man and beast,

My reason.

And Panthea, instead of admitting with Annabella that her lover has "won the field and never fought," swears that she would rather "search out death" than "welcome such a sin." Fortunately Beaumont and Fletcher rescue her from the predicament by showing that the dilemma never existed. In Brume's

Love-Sick Court the supposedly incestuous passion, which is a subsidiary element in the play, is in a similar way proved innocent by disclosures in the last act. Between Middleton's *Women Beware Women* and *'Tis Pity* there is a very considerable parallelism of situation; in both plays there is a group of uncle, nephew and servant engaged in the courtship of a woman already involved in criminal relations with a near kinsman. But parallelism of treatment there is not. For one thing, the criminal relationship is entered upon in partial ignorance of its nature; for another, there is not the slightest attempt to idealize the character of the union. The play is constructed by a realist who is interested in showing how crime punishes itself by natural laws. In the *Unnatural Combat*— of which the title alone suggests a significant difference from *' Tis Pity*— Massinger presents a situation similar to that of Shelley's *Cenci,* and treats it with artistic seriousness and the most uncompromising moral severity. He prepares the way for Malefort's ultimate degradation by making him the poisoner of his wife and the murderer of his son before he becomes the lover of his daughter. And yet he makes even Malefort shudder before his last temptation and clearly recognize its character: Malefort, infinitely wickeder and wiser than Giovanni, says in so many words that the torch which kindles his wild desires was not lighted at Cupid's altars, but was thrown into his bosom from hell. Vile though he is, he possesses the moral vision and candor of the Shakesperean villain. His passion, needless to say, is not reciprocated. He dies, not like Giovanni resolute and unshaken in his sinister idealism but rather like Marlowe's Faustus, in terrific moral agony, cursing his " cause of being." The tragedy ends with a tremendous vindication of " the sacred laws of God and man prophaned"; the last speech of Malefort is cut short by a thunderbolt which kills him. That flash of lightning may fairly be considered as Massinger's comment on incest — a comment, on the whole, rather more illuminating and salutary than the tearful

couplet in which Ford's Cardinal bids a compassionate adieu to Annabella.

This examination of plays related in subject to ' Tis Pity serves but to emphasize Ford's independence of his English contemporaries so far as treatment is concerned. I have, nevertheless, taken pains to say that his attitude toward incestuous passion is without precedent in *English* drama. It is not without precedent in Italian drama. I refer to a play which so far as I know has never been employed to explain ' Tis Pity— *Canace e I Macareo,* a tragedy written on classical models by Sperone Speroni, a distinguished critic, orator, and poet of the sixteenth century. If, as Professor Schelling asserts, Ford did indeed show a remarkable " freedom from the influence of Italian models,"' the analogies between these two plays, both in plot and in treatment, are surprising. If Ford did not write with a knowledge of Speroni's work, he at least wrote thoroughly in the spirit of it. It may even be said, I think without danger of contradiction, that *Canace e Macareo* is a more *Elisabcthan Drama,* vol. n, p. 333. The statement may have been influenced by Koeppel, *£iucllen-&tudien,* p. I 76: *"Ford's litc-rarisches Lebenswerk in fast ganz fret.von italicnischen EinJIiisscn."* plausible "source" for ' Tis Pity than anything that has been proposed heretofore.

The Italian play is a humanized dramatization of a myth treated by Ovid in *Heroides,* xi, a frequent point of reference for Elizabethan casuists. The theme is the tragical ending of the incestuous loves of Canace and Macareo, the fair son and daughter of Eolo (£olus). As in ' Tis Pity, their criminal intercourse is revealed by its unhappy fruit. On discovering the state of affairs, Eolo forces his daughter to kill herself, Macareo takes his own life. As in ' Tis Pity, the lovers die amid the suspended gayety of a birthday celebration. The nurse of Canace corresponds accurately in function to the "tutoress" of Annabella; the servant of Macareo corresponds roughly to the confessor of Giovanni; and there are some other minor correspondences.

The really striking parallelism, however, is in the treatment. Speroni, like Ford, bends all his energies to the task of soliciting pity and admiration for the unnatural lovers. He, too, insists that they are driven on not by lust but by fate or divine foreordering:

Ma quel vero tntelletto, che dal cielo
Alia rncntr materna
Mostra in sogno il mio error sotto alcun Telo,
Sa bien chc 'l mio peccato,
Non malizia mortale,
Ma fu celeste forza,
Che ogni nostra virtu vince ed ammorza.

He, too, makes his hero a Renaissance Platonist, identifying the good and the beautiful and the worship of beauty with the love of virtue. Macareo, like Giovanni, regards his love as a proof of his intelligence:

Amu infinitamente e volentieri
Le bellezze, i costumi, e le virtuti
Di mia sorella, e parmi
Che indegnamente degno
Saria di sentimento e di ragione,
Chi si rare eccellenze non amasse,
Ovunque ei le trovasse.

When danger threatens, Macareo is ready to rush on death without fear, for the fatal blade will release from the erring flesh his immaculate soul *Fanima im-maculata).* In the other world he hopes to be reunited to his sister; even the verbal parallelism is close here. Anticipating Giovanni's

Where'er I go, let me enjoy this grace,
Freely to view my Annabella's face

Macareo says:

In eterno vivra l'anima mia:
E fia suo paradiso
II poter vagheggiare
L'ombra del suo bel viso.

Both lovers die unrepentant and in unshaken loyalty to each other. Canace, on her deathbed, says that her one consolation is the knowledge that her name and face will live in the heart of her brother, to whom she sends this message:

Moriamo volentieri,
Tu per esser fedele, io per amare.

This is precisely the spirit of Annabella's

Che morte piu dolce che morire per amore?

After the death of the children, Eolo repents of his part in it, and declares that he has earned for himself eternal infamy by ending the lives of those whose only fault was that they loved. For, says he, " present and future times, forgetting their amorous errors, will blame only my cruelty." Here Eolo anticipates the opinion of Giovanni,

If ever after-times should hear
Of our fast-knit affections, though perhaps
The laws of conscience and of civil use
May justly blame us, yet when they but know
Our loves, that love will wipe away that rigour
Which would in other incests be abhorred.

Canace e Macareo seems to have impressed Speroni'g contemporaries much as ' *Tis Pity* impresses us to-day; for in the polite and learned circles of sixteenth century Italy it produced a critical controversy as interesting as the play itself. The summaries and fragments of the lectures in defense of the tragedy delivered in the *Acca-demia degli Elevati* in Padua are particularly illuminating, because they express substantially what Ford would probably have said had he been challenged to defend ' *Tis Pity.* Since it is by no means impossible that Ford knew Speroni's defense as well as his drama, it may not be amiss briefly to suggest the nature of his arguments.' Sperone Speroni was born in 1500 and died in 1588. As » young man he was professor of logic at Padua. In 1528 he resigned his chair and devoted himself to a life of scholarly leisure. In I 546 the first authentic edition of *Canace* was published. This tragedy gave rise to a critical controversy which continued inter-mittingly till 1590. Speroni was also author of numerous critical treatises and dialogues on language, love, ladies, etc. , and was a copious correspondent with Italian poets and men of letters. In 1551 eight of the dialogues were translated into French. (Upon the considerable fame and influence of Speroni in France see *Les Sources Italiennes de la " Deffense et Illustration de la Langue Francoise"* Pierre Villey, Paris, 1908.) Professor Spingarn informs me that there are " constant allusions to him in the earlier French criticism — *e.g.,* La Mesnardiere, *Poetijue,* 1640 "; it seems probable that English acquaintance with him in the seventeenth century was frequently second hand. The earliest English reference that 1 find is in Coryat's *Cruditses,* 1611. Coryat describes the statue of Speroni in the Palace at Padua and transcribes the Latin epitaph beneath it. At this time, says Coryat, there were 1500 students at the university — among them many Englishmen. Later references and allusions may be found in Sir William Alexander's *Anacrisis,* ? 1634 (Spingarn's *Critical Essays of the Seventeenth Century,* s, 185); Butler's *Upon Critics,* ? 1678 *(Critical Essays,* n, 280); Rymer's *Tragedies of the Last Age,* 1678 (page 77 in the second edition, 1691) —Rymer gives the plot of *Canace* at some length and discusses it; Dryden's *Sylvae,* 1685 (Ker's *Essays of John Dryden,* s,

The weightiest charge against *Canace e Macareo* was that the chief characters, being thoroughly vicious *(scelerate),* had according to Aristotelian canons no place in tragedy. To this the reply is made that they actually appeared in tragedy of Aristotle's day, and that they are not thoroughly vicious, but middling characters, neither perfectly good nor perfectly bad. In this connection, Speroni reminds his hearers of two arguments urged by Dejopeja, wife of Eolo. The children did not deserve death, she maintained, first, because they had merely done *per forza* what the gods do *per volont a* in heaven; second, because they had done that in the Iron Age which was permitted in the innocent Age of Gold. This position is supported by a multitude of references to the poets. Then, glancing at the customs of the ancient Persians and Egyptians, Speroni comes to a point of distinct coincidence with Ford, namely, that the union of brother and sister is forbidden not by nature but by the laws, and not even by all laws. Therefore, as the example of the best poets proves, things done under the influence of immeasurable love are not to be classed as criminal. " It may be objected," he says in substance, " that I myself have in the play called the lovers *scelerate*. Not so; do not confound me with the persons of the tra-gedy."

In his second lecture Speroni attempts to prove that pity falls justly in every case upon those who have suffered for love. To defend this position he resorts to exactly that form of romantic logic which we observed in Ford's youthful pamphlets and later in the mouth of Giovanni. It is the privilege of unfortunate lovers to be pitied; for love is the desire of beauty. The recognition of beauty is the function of man which distinguishes him from the brute. It is peculiar to man to recognize and delight in beauty, because it is the function of reason. For beauty consists in proportion, and agreement and order of the parts; but where these exist, there are also *prius* and *posterius* and *antecedens* and *consequens;* and these things can be recognized only by the reason. Therefore man alone knows beauty, and exhibits his reason by delighting in it. It is, in short, the privilege of unfortunate lovers to be pitied, because they have come to grief through the exercise of their highest faculty. To make the contention specific, "the love of the twins of the tragedy is not *disonesto,*" because the " love of country and of glory is not so peculiar to a human being as that love which is desire of beauty. Therefore, sin caused by this latter is more human, because this species is found only in man; but the other two are found also in other animals."

I have dwelt at considerable length upon the tragedy and the criticism of the " Plato " of the Paduan academy because in this forgotten Italian material are to be found the full illustration and the explicit theory of every singular characteristic in Ford's most individual play. Here is the Platonic theology of love — its logic, its insistence upon the inviolability of the soul, itsmystical reverence of passion, and its earnest fatalism — seriously applied to the extenu-

ation of hideous crime and to the glorification of the criminals. If *Canace e Macareo* was not the direct source of ' *Tis Pity,* it was at any rate a noteworthy tributary to that stream of bewildering and dangerous neo-pagan ideas which flowed into England from Italy, and made the production of ' *Tis Pity* possible. The decadent and vicious idealism of both of these tragedies — this is perhaps sufficient justification for considering them attentively — is the fruit of the general moral and intellectual emancipation of the Renaissance.

From this survey of Ford's work it should appear plainly enough that he was not one of the myriad-minded and puissant men of the age, to whom nothing human was alien. It seems as if temperament, culture, and the time-spirit had conspired to make him a writer of originality and power only within extremely narrow limits. I have said that his reputation rests upon his three tragedies, and one of them, *Lovis Sacrifice,* is a failure. It would scarcely be going too far to say that no contributive tendency and no excellence of artistic achievement peculiarly his would be ignored if he were remembered only by the two plays included in this volume. Here are his best plots; all but one — Bianca — of his memorable characters; his sweetest poetry; his fundamental and creative ideas. His amorous and melancholic temperament tended to restrict his outlook, even from youth, to the field of love and sexual passion. His reading in the romantic literature of the last quarter of the sixteenth century confirmed his natural bent, and added to his emotions whatever intellectual content was possessed by the Platonic theology of love. If his legal training affected his literary processes, I suspect we may discover traces of its influence in the proclivity of his characters for deciding cases of conscience on grounds of equity and natural reason. *As* a lawyer he may easily have learned a certain disrespect for the law in so far as it is a body of rules based upon social expediency rather than upon absolute justice. Furthermore, he found a curious corroboration of the scholastic fatalism and ratio-

nalism of his youth in the medical rationalism of Burton. All these forces, bearing upon a mind as earnest and as humorless as Shelley's, produced in Ford a disdain for vulgar orthodoxy, and made him a romantic rationalist in morals. After a generation of great dramatists had spoken, he had still something to say. He had to say that the essence of tragedy is the defeat of the ideal by the real world. In order to explain the idea dramatically he had to invent the problem play. If he could have supported his theory of tragedy by a series of such fine and effective illustrations as the *Broken Heart,* he would have made himself a large and secure place in literature. Unfortunately, however, his experience, judgment, and common sense were unequal to the task. His talent was limited by a morbid temperament. His intellectual grasp was weak when he wrote *Love's Sacrifice.* When he wrote ' *Tis Pity,* though every artistic faculty was alert, he was deserted by common-sense.

THE TEXT

The text here printed follows the first and only seventeenth-century edition, the quarto of 1633. Dyce discovered two or three minute differences in the copies he examined; but there seems to have been no second quarto edition of any play produced by Ford independently. The quarto has been compared with Weber's edition in the *Dramatic Works of John Ford,* 1811, and with the Gifford-Dyce edition in the *fforks of John Ford,* 1895. Weber's notoriously defective edition was a lively provocative to accuracy in Gifford's edition of 1827. But though Gifford decisively superseded Weber, his own editorial work was by no means flawless, and he permitted himself editorial licenses no longer approved. For the revised edition of 1869 Dyce thoroughly overhauled Gifford's text, comparing it with various copies of the quartos, and restoring original readings or noting them among the variants. The 1895 edition is a reissue "with further additions" by A. H. Bullen. There still remain some needless corrections, numerous expansions of colloquial contractions, and changes in the stage directions. In the present editions variants of Gifford-Dyce (G-D) are recorded when they are of interest or importance to the text.

The spelling of the quarto has been restored, except that the old forms of *j,* j, and *v* have not been retained, and obvious misprints — such as an » for a *u* — have been silently corrected. Capitalization and punctuation have been modernized, and commas have been substituted for the characteristic parentheses enclosing the nominative of direct address. Changes or additions in the text are indicated by brackets or foot-notes or both. The name of each character is printed in full at his first appearance in each scene, and then is uniformly abbreviated without reference to sporadic variations. The division and placing of the scenes is based on that of the Gifford-Dyce edition.

Pitty Shee $ a W tiore

Aded by the *Queenes* Maiefties Seruants, at The Thanix In L 0

Printed *y Collins,* and are to be fold at his fhop in *Pault* Church-yard, acthe figne ofihethreeKings. 1633.

SOURCES

No perfectly certain source of this play has been discovered. Events in some respects similar to those of the tragedy are said to have taken place in Normandy in 1603. An account of them is given by the chronicler Pierre Matthieu in his *Histoirc dc France et des Choses Memorable ...,* published in Paris, 1606. The story is retold by Francois de Rosset in *Let Histoircs Tragiyues de Nostrc Temps.* It is the fifth tale in the second edition, 1615; the seventh in the edition of 1619. Wolff declares outright that Ford took his plot from this source. (See *John Forde ein Nachamer Shakespeare's,* page 8). But Koeppel approves Dyce's observation that" though Ford may probably have read it, there are no particular resemblances between it and the play." (See Koeppel's *Quellen-Studien,* page 180; also, Gifford-Dyce, Introduction, page xxx.)

A great part of the Shakesperean influence which Wolff attempted to trace in this play is purely imaginary. It is not difficult, however, to see a certain general likeness between Friar Bonaven-tu-ra and Friar Laurence, and — to a less degree —-between other characters of *'Tis Pity* and *Romeo and Juliet.*

As a possible indirect source W. Bang and H. de Vocht suggest the Ilepl *ipwTsKws'* Traftj/udTux of Parthenios of Nikaia. See *Englische Studicn,* Band 36, pp. 391-93 (1906).

There is a striking parallelism — hitherto, I think, unnoticed — between Annabella, Donado, Bergetto, and Poggio; and Isabella, Guardiano, the Ward, and Sordido in Middleton's *Women Beware Women.* The resemblance is the more worth noting as the same element of unnatural passion enters into the intrigue of both plays.

In my introduction 1 have discussed at some length an impressive analogue and possible source of *'Tis Pity* in Speroni's *Canacc e Macareo.* TO THE TRITELY NOBLE, JOHN EARLE OF PETERBOROUGH, LORD MORDANT, BARON OF TURVEY

My Lord,

Where a truth of meritt hath a generall warrant, there love is but a debt, acknowledgement a justice. Greatnesse cannot often claime virtue by inheritance j yet in this, yours appeares most eminent, for that you are not more rightly heyre to your fortunes, then glory shalbe to your memory. Sweetenesse of disposition ennobles a freedome of birth; in both, your lawfull interest adds honour to your owne name, and mercy to my presumption. Your noble allowance of these first fruites of my leasure in the action, emboldens my confidence of your as noble construction in this presentment: especially since my service must ever owe particular duty to your favours, by a particular ingagement. The gravity of the subject may easily excuse the leightnesse of the title: otherwise, I had beene a severe judge against mine owne guilt. Princes have vouchsaf t grace to trifles, offred from a purity of devotion; your Lordship may likewise please to admit into your good opinion, with these weake endeavours, the constancy of affection from the, sincere lover of your deserts in honour.

JOHN FORD.
The Sceane.
PARMA
THE ACTORS' NAMES.
Bonaventura, a fryar.
A Cardinali., nuntio to the Pop.
Soranzo, a nobleman.
Florio, a cittizen of Parma.
Donado, another cittizen.
Grimaldi, a Roman gentleman.
Giovanni, sonne to Florio.
Bergetto, nephew to Donado.
Richardetto, a suppos'd phisitian.
Vasques, servant to Soranzo.
Poggio, servant to Bergetto.
Bandetti.
Woemen
Annabella, daughter to Florio.
Hippolita, wife to Richardetto.
Philotis, his neece.
Putana, tutresse to Annabella.
Officers, Attendants, Servants, 5tc.
T/ie Scians. In the quarto this page immatcljr followe Che title-page.
ACTUS PRIMUS. SCENA PRIMA. *Friar Bonaventura's «//. Enter Fryar and Giovanni. Fryar.* Dispute no more in this; for know, young man,
These are no schoole-points; nice philosophy
May tolerate unlikely arguments,
But heaven admits no jest; wits that presum'd
On wit too much, — by striving how to prove
There was no God, — with foolish grounds of art
Discover'd first the neerest way to hell,
And fild the world with develish atheisms:
Such questions, youth, are fond; for better 'tis
To blesse the sunne then reason why it shines;
Yet hee thou talk'st of is above the sun.
No more; I may not heare it.
Giovanni. Gentle father,
To you I have unclasp't my burthened soule, Empty'd the store-house of my thoughts and heart, 9/or. G-D, far.
Made my selfe poore of secrets; have not left 15
Another word untold, which hath not

spoke
All what I ever durst or thinke or know;
And yet is here the comfort I shall have,
Must I not doe what all men else may,
—love?
Fry. Yes, you may love, faire sonne.
Gio. Must I not praise »o
That beauty which, if fram'd a new, the gods
Would make a god of, if they had it there,
And kneele to it, as I doe kneele to them?
Fry. Why, foolish madman,— *Gio.*
Shall a peevish sound,
    A customary forme, from man to man, »5
    Of brother and of sister, be a barre
Twixt my perpetuall happinesse and mee?
Say that we had one father, say one wombe —
Curse to my joyes —gave both us life and birth;
Are wee not therefore each to other bound *y*
    So much the more by nature, by the links
Of blood, of reason, — nay, if you will hav't,—
Even of religion, to be ever one,
One soule, one flesh, one love, one heart, one all?
Fry. Have done, unhappy youth, for thou art lost. 35 *Gio.* Shall, then, for that I am her brother borne, My joyes be ever banisht from her bed? No, father; in your eyes I see the change
    Of pitty and compassion; from your age,
    As from a sacred oracle, distills 40
    The life of counsell: tell mee, holy man,
    What cure shall give me ease in these extreames.
Fry. Repentance, sonne, and sorrow for this sinne:
For thou hast mov'd a Majesty above
With thy un-raunged almost blasphemy. 45
Gio. O, doe not speake of that, deare confessor!
Fry. Art thou, my sonne, that miracle of wit Who once, within these three moneths, wert esteem'd

A wonder of thine age throughout Bononia?
How did the University applaud
Thy goverment, behaviour, learning, speech,
Sweetnesse, and all that could make up a man!
I was proud of my tutellage, and chose
Rather to leave my bookes then part withthee;
I did so: but the fruites of all my hopes 55
    Are lost in thee, as thou art in thy selfe.
O, Giovanni! hast thou left the schooles
Of knowledge to converse with lust and death?
For death waites on thy lust. Looke through
the world,
    And thou shalt see a thousand faces shine 6a
    More glorious then this idoll thou ador'st:
    Leave her, and take thy choyce, 'tis much lesse sinne; Though in such games as those, they lose that winne.
Gio. It were more ease to stop the ocean
From floates and ebbs then to disswade my i vowes. 65 *Fry.* Then I have done, and in thy wilfull flames
Already see thy ruine; heaven is just,
Yet heare my counsell.
Gio. As a voyce of life.
Fry. Hye to thy fathers house, there locke thee fast
Alone within thy chamber, then fall downe 70
On both thy knees, and grovell on the ground:
Cry to thy heart, wash every word thou utter'st
In teares, — and if't bee possible, — of blood:
Begge heaven to cleanse the leprosie of lust
That rots thy soule, acknowledge what thou art, 75
A wretch, a worme, a nothing: weepe, sigh, p'ray
Three times a day and three times every night:
For seven dayes space doe this; then if thou
find'st

No change in thy desires, returne to me:
I'le thinke on remedy. Pray for thy selfe 80
    At home, whil'st I pray for thee here. Away!
My blessing with thee. Wee have neede to pray!
Gio. All this I'le doe, to free mee from the rod
Of vengeance; else I'lesweare my fate's my god.
Exeunt.

SCENA SECUNDA.

The street before Florio's house. Enter Grimaldi and Vasques ready to Fight.
Vasques. Come, sir, stand to your tackling; if you prove craven, I'le make you run quickly.
Grimaldi. Thou art no equall match for mee. *Vas.* Indeed, I never went to the warres to bring home newes; nor cannot play the moun-5 tibanke for a meales meate, and sweare I got my wounds in the field. See you these gray haires? They'le not flinch for a bloody nose. Wilt thou to this geere? *Gri.* Why, slave, think'st thou I'le ballance 10 my reputation with a cast-suite? Call thy mais-ter; he shall know that I dare —
Vas. Scold like a cot-queane, — that's your profession. Thou poore shaddow of a souldier, I will make thee know my maister keepes ser-15 vants thy betters in quality and performance. Com'st thou to fight or prate? *Gri.* Neither, with thee; I am a Romane and a gentleman, one that have got mine honour with ex-pence of blood. ao *Vas.* You are a lying coward and a foole! iS-zo *Neither... bind.* Q prints as verse.
Fight, or, by these hilts, I'le kill thee, — brav«
my lord! — you'le fight.
Gri. Provoake me not, for if thou dost
—
Vas. Have at you
They fight; Grimal. hath the worst.
Enter Florio, Donado, Soranzo.
Florio. What meaned these sudden broyles so
neare my dores? »$
    Have you not other places but my house
To vent the spleene of your disordered

bloods?

Must I be haunted still with such unrest
As not to eate or sleepe in peace at home?

Is this your love, Grimaldi? Fie, 't is naught, je

Donado. And, Vasques, I may tell thee, 'tis
not well
To broach these quarrels; you are ever forward
In seconding contentions.

Enter above Annabella and Putana.

Flo. What's the ground?

Soranzo. That, with your patience, signiors,
I'le resolve:
This gentleman, whom fame reports a soul-
dier,— 35
For else I know not, — rivals mee in love
To Signior Florio's daughter; to whose eares
He still preferrs his suite to my disgrace,
15 *mtaned.* G-D, mean.
Thinking the way to recommend himselfe
Is to disparage me in his report: 40
But know, Grimaldi, though, may be, thou art
My equall in thy blood, yet this be-
wrayes
A lownesse in thy minde; which, wer't thou noble,
Thou would'st as much disdaine as I doe thee
."or this unworthinesse; and on this ground 45
I will'd my servant to correct his tongue,
Holding a man so base no match for me.

Vas. And had not your sudd en comming prevented us, I had let my gentleman blood under the gilles; I should
have worm'd you, sir, for 50 running madde.

Gri. He be reveng'd, Soranzo. *Vas.* On a
dish of warme-broth to stay your stom-
ack—doe, honest innocence, doe!
Spone-rneat is a wholesomer dyet then a
Spannish blade. 55 *Gri.* Remember this!
Sor. I feare thee not, Grimaldi. *Ex. Gri.*
Flo. My Lord Soranzo, this is strange to

me, Why you should storme, having my
word en- gag'd;
Owing her heart, what neede you doubt
her eare? may talke by law of any game.
60 46 *Aii. Q,* this. 48 *iuddin.* g, tudda ne.
Vas. Yet thevillaine of words, Signior
Florio, maybe such as would make any
unspleen'd dove chollerick; blame not
my lord in this. *Flo.* Be you more silent;
I would not for my wealth, my daugh-
ters love 65 Should cause the spilling
of one drop of blood. Vasques, put up:
let's end this fray in wine.

Exeunt, Putana. How like you this,
child? Here's threatning, challenging,
quarrelling, and fighting on every side,
and all is for your sake; you had neede
looke to your selfe, chardge; you'le be
stolne away sleeping else shortly.
Annabella. But, tutresse, such a life
gives no content
To me; my thoughts are fixt on other
ends. Would you would leave me! j *Put.*
Leave you? No marvaile else; leave me
no leaving, chardge. This is love outright. In-deede, I blame you not; you
have choyce fit for the best lady in Italy.
Anna. Pray doe not talke so much. f,
Put. Take the worst with the best,
there's Gri-maldi the souldier, a very
well-timbred fellow: they say he is a
Roman, nephew to the Duke Mount
Ferratto; they say he did good service
in the warrs against the Millanoys; but,
faith, 85 chardge, I doe not like him, and
be for nothing 61-3 2 prints u Tcik. but
for being a souldier: one amongst twenty of your skirmishing captaines but
have some pryvie mayme or other that
marres their standing upright. I like him
the worse, hee crinckles 90 so much in
the hams; though hee might serve if
their were no more men, — yet hee's
not the man I would choose. *Anna.* Fye,
how thou prat'st! *Put.* As I am a very
woman, I like Sfgniour 95 Soranzo
well: hee is wise, and what is more,
rich; and what is more then that, kind;
and what is more then all this, a nobleman; such a one, were I the faire
Annabella my selfe, I would wish and
pray for. Then hee is bounti-ioo full;
besides, hee is handsome, and, by my
troth, I thinke, wholsome — and that's
newes in a gallant of three and twenty;

liberall, that I know; loving, that you
know; and a man sure, else hee could
never ha' purchast such a good name
with 105 Hippolita, the lustie widdow,
in her husbands life time. And 'twere
but for that report, sweet heart, would
'a were thine! Commend a man for his
qualities, but take a husband as he is
a plaine-sufficient, naked man: such a
one is forno your bed, and such a one
is Signior Soranzo, my life for't. *Anna.*
Sure the woman tooke her mornings
draught to soone. *Enter Bergetts and
Poggio.* *Put.* But looke, sweet heart,
looke what thinge n conies now! Here's
another of your cyphers to fill up the
number: Oh, brave old ape in a silken
coate! Observe. *Ber.* Dids't thou thinke,
Poggio, that I would spoyle my new
cloathes, and leave my dinner to no
fight? *Pog.* No, sir, I did not take you
for so arrant a babie. *Ber.* I am wyser
then so: for I hope, Poggio, thou never
heard'st of an elder brother that was 125
a coxcombe; dids't, Poggio? *Pog.* Never,
indeede, sir, as long as they had either
land or mony left them to inherit. *Ber.*
Is it possible, Poggio? Oh, monstruous!
Why, He undertake with a handfull of
silver 10130 buy a headfull of wit at any
tyme: but, sirrah, I have another purchase in hand. I shall have the wench,
myne unckle sayes. I will but wash my
face, and shift socks, and then have at
her, yfaith... Marke my pace, Poggio!
135 *Pog.* Sir, I have seene an asse and a
mule trot the Spannish pavin with a better grace, I know not how often. *Exeunt.*
Anna. This ideot haunts me too. *Put.* I,
I, he needes no discription. The rich 140
magnifico that is below with your father, chardge,
Signior Donado his unckle, for that he
meanes to make this, his cozen, a gold-
en calfe, thinkes ihat you wil be a right
Isralite, and. fall downe to him presently: but I hope I have tuterd you 145 better. They say a fooles bable is a ladies
playfellow; yet you, having wealth
enough, you neede not cast upon the
dearth of flesh at any rate. Hang him, innocent!

Enter Giovanni. *Anna.* But see, Putana,
see! What blessed shape 150
Of some caelestiall creature now ap-

peares!
What atan is hee that with such sad aspect
Walkes carelesse of him selfe?
Put. Where?
Anna. Looke below. *Put.* Oh, 'tis your brother, sweet. *Anna.* Ha! *Put.* 'Tis your brother. *Anna.* Sure 'tis not hee; this is some woefull thinge 155
Wrapt up in griefe, some shaddow of a man.
Alas, hee beats his brest, and wipes his eyes,
Drown'dall inteares: me thinkes I heare him sigh.
Lets downe, Putana, and pertake the cause.
I know my brother in the love he beares me 'o
Will not denye me partage in his sadnesse —
soule is full of heavinesse and feare.
Exit above with Putana. SCENA TERTIA.
' A hall in Fiono's house.
Giovanni. Lost! I am lost! my fates have dootn'd mv__death:
The more I striveTllove; the more I love,
The-lesse I hope: I see my mine certaine.
What judgement or endevors' could apply
To my incurable and restlesse wounds, 5
I throughly have examin'd, but in vaine.
0 that it were not in religion sinne
To make our love a god, and worship it!
1 have even wearied heaven with prayers, dryed P
The spring of my continuall teares, even sterv'd 10
My veines with dayly fasts: what wit or art
Could counsaile, I have practiz'd; but, alas,
I find all these but dreames and old mens
tales
To fright unsteedy youth; I'me still the same:
Or I must speake or burst; tis not, I know, «tj
My lust, but 'tis my fate that leads me

on., .'.
Keepe feare and low faint hearted shame with
slaves!
I'le tell her that I love her, though my heart
Were rated at the price of that attempt.
Oh me! she comes.
Enter Anna, and Putana. Annabella. Brother!
Gio. aside. If such a thing »o
As courage dwell In men, yee heavenly powers,
Now double all that virtue in my tongue!
Anna. Why, brother,
Will you not speake to me?
Gio. Yes: how d'ee, sister?
Anna. Howsoever I am, me thinks you are not well. 15 *Putana.* Blesse us! why are you so sad, sir? *Gio.* Let me intreat you, leave us awhile, Putana.
Sister, I would be pryvate with you.
Anna. With-drawe, Putana. *Put.* I will.
— *Aside.* If this were any 30 / other company for her, I should thinke my absence an office of some credit; but I will leave them together. *Exit Putana.* —/
Gio. Come, sister, lend your hand: let's walke together.
I hope you neede not blush to walke with mee; 35 Here's none but you and I.
Anna. How's this? *Gio.* Faith,
I meane no harme.
Anna. Harme? *Gio.* No, good faith.
How is't with 'ee?
Anna. I trust hee be not franticke —
I am very well, brother.
Gio. Trust me, but I am sicke: I feare so sick
'Twill cost my life.
Anna. Mercy forbid it! 'tis not so, I hope. *Gio.* I thinke you love me, sister.
Anna. Yes, you know
I doe.
Gio. I know't, indeed — y'are very faire. *Anna.* Nay, then, I see you have a merry sicknesse..-, / *Gie.* That's as it proves: the poets aigne, I read,
That Juno for her forehead did exceede
All other goddesses; but I durst sweare
Your forehead exceeds hers, as hers did theirs.
Anna. Troth, this is pretty!
Gio. Such a paire of starres 50

As are thine eyes would, like Promethean fire,
If gently glaun'st, give life to senselesse stones.
Anna. Fie upon 'ee!
Gio. The lilly and the rose, most sweetly strainge, Upon your dimpled cheekes doe strive for change. 55 Such lippes would tempt a saint; such hands as 44 / *Joe.* Q prints with line above. 46 *the.* Q, *they.* 49 *than.* G, theirs. D, their. those Would make an anchoret lascivious.
Anna. D'ee mock mee or flatter mee?
Gio. If you would see a beauty more exact Then art can counterfit or nature frame, o
Looke in your glasse, and there behold your owne.
Anna. O, you are a trime youth. *Gio.* Here! *Offers his dagger to her. Anna.* What to doe? *Gio.* And here's my breast; strike home! Rip up my bosome; there thou shalt behold A heart in which is writ the truth I speake. 65 Why stand 'ee? *Anna.* Are you earnest? *Gio.* Yes, most earnest.
You cannot love?
Anna. Whom? *Gio.* Me! My tortur'd soule
Hath felt affliction in the heate of death —
O Annabella, I am quite undone!
The love of thee, my sister, and the view 7
Of thy immortall beauty hath untun'd
All harmony both of my rest and life.
Why d'ee not strike?
63 ttrihi. Q, strick.
Anna. Forbid it, my just feares!
If this be true, 'twere fitter I were dead.
Gio. True, Annabella; 'tis no time to jest. 75 I have too long supprest the hidden flames That almost have consum'd me: I have spent Many a silent night in sighes and groanes, Ran over all my thoughts, despis'd my fate, Reason'd against the reasons of my love, 80
Done all that smooth'd-cheeke vertue could advise;
But found all bootelesse: 'tis my destiny
That you must eyther love, or I must dye.
Anna. Comes this in sadnesse from you?

Gio. Let some mischiefe
Befall me soone, if I dissemble ought.
g- *Anna.* You are my brother, Giovanni.
Gio. You,
My sister Annabella; I know this,
And could afford you instance why to love
So much the more for this; to which intent
Wise nature first in your creation ment *ye*
   To make you mine; else't had beene sinne and foule
   To share one beauty to a double soule.
Neerenesse in birth or blood doth but perswade
A neerer neerenesse in affection.
I have askt counsell of the holy church, 95
Who tells mee I may love you; and 'tis just
That, since I may, I shou/d; and will, yes,
81 *unooth'd-chakt.* Altered by G to smooth-cheek'd. 93 *or.* G-D, and.
will!
Must I now live or dye?
Anna. Live; thou hast wonne
The field, and never fought; what thou hast urg'd
   My captive heart had Jong agoe resolv'd. o
   I blush to tell thee, — but I'le tell thee now,—
For every sigh that thou hast spent for me
I have sigh'd ten; for every teare shed twenty:
And not so much for that I lov'd, as that I durst not say I lov'd, nor scarcely thinke it. 105
Gio. Let not this musicke be a dreame, yee gods, For pittie's-sake, I begge 'ee.
Anna. On my knees, *Sbee kneeles.*
Brother, even by our mothers dust, I charge you,
   Doe not betray mee to your mirth or hate:
Love mee or kill me, brother.
Gio. On my knees, *He kneeles. no*
   Sister, even by my mothers dust, I charge you,
Doe not betray mee to your mirth or hate:

Love mee or kill mee, sister.
Anna. You meane good sooth, then?
Gio. In good troth, I doe;
And so doe you, I hope: say, I'm in earnest. 115 *Anna.* Fle swear't, and I.
Gio. And I; and by this kisse,-
Kisses her.
Once more! yet once more! now let's rise, —
by this,
   I would not change this minute for Elyzium.
What must we now doe? HMWl M«3
Anna. What you will.
Gio. Come, then;
   After so many teares as wee have wept,,
   Let's learne to court in smiles, to kisse and sleepe. *Exeunt.* SCENA QUARTA. *J street. Enter Florio and Donado.*
Florio. Signior Donado, you have sayd enough —
   I understand you; but would have you know
I will not force my daughter 'gainst her will.
You see I have but two, a sonne and her;
And hee is so devoted to his booke, 5
   As I must tell you true, I doubt his health:
Should he miscarry, all my hopes rely
Upon my girle. As for worldly fortune,
I am, I thanke my starres, blest with enough.
My care is how to match her to her liking: lo
v Il6 *I' It tutor' t, and I.* G-D, I'll (wear it, I.
   I would not have her marry wealth, but love;
And if she like your nephew, let him have her.
Here's all that I can say.
Donado. Sir, you say well,
   Like a true father; and, for my part, I,
If the young folkes can like,— twixt you and
me,— 15
   Will promise to assure my nephew presently
Three thousand florrens yeerely during life,
And after I am dead my whole estate.
Flo. "Tis a faire proffer, sir, meant-time your nephew

Shall have free passage to commence his suite: «
If hee can thrive, hee shall have my consent.
So for this time I'le leave you, signior. *Exit.*
Do. Well,
   Here's hope yet, if my nephew would have wit;
   But hee is such another dunce, I feare Hee'le never winne the wench. When I was
young,
   I could have done't, yfaith; and so shall hee,
If hee will learne of mee; and, in good time,
Hee comes himselfe.
Enter Bergetto and Poggio.
How now, Bergetto, whether away so fast?
Bergetto. Oh, unkle, I have heard the strangest 30 newes that ever came out of the mynt 1 Have I not, Poggio?
29 *How now... fut f Q* gives this to Poggio. *Poggio.* Yes, indeede, sir. *Do.* What newes, Bergetto? *Ber.* Why, looke yee, unkle, my barber told 35 me just now that there is a fellow come to towne who undertakes to make a mill goe with-out the mortall helpe of any water or winde, onely with sand-bags: and this fellow hath a strange horse, a most excellent beast, I'le assure 40 you, unkle, my barber sayes, whose head to the wonder of all Christian people, stands just behind where his tayle is — is "t not true, Poggio? *Pog.* So the barber swore, forsooth. *Do.* And you are running thither? 45 *Ber.* I, forsooth, unkle. *Do.* Wilt thou be a foole stil? Come, sir, you shall not goe. You have more mind of a puppet-play then on the businesse I told y 'ee. Why, thou great baby, wu't never have wit? 50 Wu't make thy selfe a May-game to all the world? *Pog.* Answere for your selfe, maister. *Ber.* Why, unkle, shu'd I sit at home still, and not goe abroad to see fashions like other 55 gallants? *Do.* To see hobby-horses! What wise talkc, 45 ' supplied by G-D.
I pray, had you with Annabella, when you were at Signior Florio's house?
Ber. Oh, the wench! Uds sa' me, unkle, I 60 tickled her with a rare speech, that

I made her almost burst her belly with laughing. *Do.* Nay, I thinke so; and what speech vas't? *Ber.* What did I say, Poggio? 65 *Pog.* Forsooth, my maister said, that hee loved her almost as well as hee loved parmasent, and swore—I'le be sworne for him — that shee wanted but such a nose as his was, to be as pretty a young woeman as any was in Parma. *Do.* Oh, grose! *Ber.* Nay, unkle, — then shee ask't mee whether my father had any more children then my selfe; and I sayd " No, 'twere better hee should have had his braynes knockt out first." 75 *Do.* This is intolerable. *Ber.* Then sayd shee, " Will Signior Donado, your unkle, leave you all his wealth?" *Do.* Ha! that was good — did she harpe upon that string? go *Ber.* Did she harpe upon that string? I, that she did. I answered,"Leave me all his wealth? Why, woeman, hee hath no other wit; if hee had, he should heare on't to his everlasting glory confusion. I know," quoth I, "I am his *i* white boy, and will not be guld." And with that she fell into a great smile, and went away. Nay, I did fit her! *Do.* Ah, sirrah, then I see there is no changing of nature. Well, Bergetto, I feare thou wilt be 90 a very asse still. *Ber.* I should be sorry for that, unkle. *Do.* Come, come you home with me: since you are no better a speaker, I'le have you write to her after some courtly manner, and inclose 95 some rich jewell in the letter. *Ber.* I, marry, that will be excellent. *Do.* Peace, innocent!
Once in my time I'le set my wits to schoole;
If all faile, 'tis but the fortune of a foole. 100
Ber. Poggio, 'twill doe, Poggio. *Exeunt.*
ACTUS SECUNDUS. SCENA PRIMA.
An apartment in Florso's house.
Enter Giovanni and Annabella as from their chamber.
Giovanni. Come, Annabella, — no more sister now, But love, a name more gracious, — doe not blush,
Beauties sweete wonder, but be proud to know
That yeelding thou hast conquer'd, and inflam'd
A heart whose tribute is thy brothers life. 5

Annabella. And mine is his! Oh, how these stolne contents
Would print a modest crymson on my cheekes, Had any but my hearts delight prevail'd!
Gio. I marvaile why the chaster of your sex Should thinke this pretty toye call'd maiden-head So strange a losse, when, being lost,'tis nothing, And you are still the same. *Anna.* 'Tis well for you;
Now you can talke.
Gio. Musicke aswell consists
In th' eare as in the playing.
Anna. Oh, y'are wanton!
Tell on't, y'are best; doe.
14 *y'art.* G-D, you're. *Gio.* Thou wilt chide me, then. 15
Kisse me — so! Thus hung Jove on Laeda's necke,
And suck't divine ambrosia from her lips.
I envy not the mightiest man alive;
But hold my selfe, in being king of thee, More great than were I king of all the world. to
But I shall lose you, sweet-heart.
Anna. But you shall not!
Gio. You must be married, mistres. *Anna.* Yes, to whom? *Gio.* Some one must have you. *Anna.* You must. *Gio.* Nay, some other. *Anna.* Now, prithee, do not speake so; without jesting You'le make me weepe in earnest. *Gio.* What, you will not! 15
But tell me, sweete, cans't thou be dar'd to sweare That thou wilt live to mee, and to no other?
Anna. By both our loves I dare; for didst thou know,
My Giovanni, how all suiters seeme
To my eyes hatefull, thou wouldst trust mee then. 30
x2 *Ton musl be married, mistret.* Q print! on line above.
11-3 *Tet... have you.* Q prints on one line. 23 *You mutt. Git. Nay, ume ot/ser.* Q prints on one line. *Gio.* Enough, I take thy word. Sweet, we must part:
Remember what thou vow'st; keepe well my heart.
Anna. Will you begon? *Gio.* I must. *Anna.* When to returne? *Gio.* Soone. *Anna.* Looke you doe. *Gio.* Farewell. *Exit. Anna.* Goe where thou wilt, in mind I 'le keepe thee here, 35

And where thou art, I know I shall be there.
Guardian!
Enter Putana. Putana. Child, how is't, child? Well,thanke heaven, ha!
Anna. O guardian, what a paradise of joy Have I past over! 40 *Put.* Nay, what a paradise of joy have you past under! Why now I commend thee, chardge. Feare nothing, sweete-heart, what though hee be your brother: your brother's a man, I hope, and I say still, if a young wench 45 feele the fitt upon her, let her take any body — father or brother, all is one. 33-4 *Will you began j Gia. I maii,* makes one line of *Q j When to returns? Gio, Soont.* another $ and *Loohs you dot. Gio.* Farewell, a third.
Anna. I would not have it knowne for all the world. *Put.* Nor I, indeed, for the speech of the people; else 'twere nothing. *Florio (within).* Daughter Annabella! *Anna.* O mee! my father. — Here, sir! — Reach my worke. *Flo. (witbin).* What are you doeing? *Anna.* So, let him come now. *Enter Florio, Ricbardetto like a Doctor of Phisiche, and Philotis witb a lute in her band. Flo.* So hard at worke! that's well; you lose no time
Looke, I have brought you company; here's one 55
A learned doctor, lately come from Padua,
Much skild in physicke; and, for that I see
You have of late beene sickly, I entreated
This reverent man to visit you some time.
Anna. Y'are very welcome, sir.
Richardetto. I thanke you, mistresse. 60
Loud fame in large report hath spoke your praise
Aswell for vertue as perfection:
For which I have beene bold to bring with mee
A kins-woeman of mine, a maide, for song
And musicke one perhaps will give content. 65
Please you to know her.
Anna. They are parts I love.
And shee for them most welcome.
Philotis. Thanke you, lady. *Flo.* Sir, now you know my house, pray make

not strange;
And if you finde my daughter neede
your art,
I'le be your pay-master.
Rich. Sir, what I am 70
Shee shall command.
Flo. You shall bind me to you.
Daughter, I must have conference with
you
About some matters that concernes us
both.
Good Maister Doctor, please you but
walke in,
Wee'le crave a little of your cozens cun-
ning: 75
I thinke my girle hath not quite forgot
To touch an instrument; she could have
don't:
Wee'le heare them both.
Rich. I'le waite upon you, sir. *Exeunt.*
SCENA SECUNDA.
*Enter Soranzo in bis study reading a
booke.*
Soranzo. Loves measure is extreame,
the com-
fort paine,
The life unrest, and the reward disdaine.
What's here? lookt o're again. 'Tis so;
so writes
This smooth licentious poet in his
rymes.
But, Sanazar, thou lyest; for had thy bo-
some 5
Felt such oppression as is laid on mine,
70-1 *Sir... command. Q* prints as one
line.
Thou wouldst have kist the rod that
made the smart.
To worke, then, happy Muse, and
contradict
What Sanazer hath in his envy writ.
*Loves measure is the meane, sweet his
annoyetj 10 His pleasures life, and his
reward all joyes.*
Had Annabella liv'd when Sanazar
Did in his briefe Encomium celebrate
Venice, that queene of citties, he had
left
That verse which gaind him such a
summe of
gold, 15
And for one onely looke from
Annabell
Had writ of her and her diviner cheekes.
O, how my thoughts are—

Basques (witbin). Pray, forbeare; in
rules of civility, let me give notice on't:
I shall be tax't 20 of my neglect of duty
and service.
Soran. What rude intrusion interrupts
my peace? Can I be no where private?
Vas. (within).Troth, you wrong your
modesty. *Soran.* What's the matter,
Vasques? who is't?
Enter HippoKta and Vasques.
Hippelita. 'Tis I: S
Doe you know mee now? Looke, perju-
rd man, on her 7 *the smart.* G-D, the e
smart. 13 *Encomium. Q,* Euconium.
Whom thou and thy distracted lust
have wrong'd.
Thy sensuall rage of blood hath made
my youth
A scorne to men and angels; and shall I
Be now a foyle to thy unsated change?
30
Thou knowst, false wanton, when my
modest fame
Stood free from staine or scandall, all
the charmes
Of hell or sorcery could not prevaile
Against the honour of my chaster bo-
some.
Thyne eyes did pleade in teares, thy
tongue in
oathes, *35*
Such and so many that a heart of
steele
Would have beene wrought to pitty, as
was mine:
And shall the conquest of my lawfull
bed,
My husbands death, urg'd on by his dis-
grace,
My losse of woeman-hood, be ill re-
warded 40
With hatred and contempt? No;
know, Soranzo,
I have a spirit doth as much distast
The slavery of fearing thee, as thou
Dost loath the memory of what hath
past.
Soran. Nay, deare Hippolita,—
Hip. Call me not deare, 45
Nor thinke with supple words to
smooth the grosenesse
Of my abuses. 'Tis not your new mis-
tresse,
Your goodly Madam Merchant, shall
triumph

On my dejection; tell her thus from
mee,
My byrth was nobler and by much more
free. 50
Soran. You are too violent.
Hip. You are too double
In your dissimulation. See'st thou this,
This habit, these blacke mourning
weedes of
care?
'Tis thou art cause of this, and hast
divorc't
My husband from his life, and me from
him, 55
And made me widdow in my widdow-
hood.
Soran. Will you yet heare?
Hip. More of the perjuries?
Thy soule is drown'd too deeply in
those sinnes; Thou needs't not add to th'
number.
Soran. Then I'le leave you.
You are past all rules of sence.
Hip. And thou of grace. 60 *Vasques.* Fy,
mistresse, you are not neere the limits
of reason: if my lord had a resolution
as noble as vertue it selfe, you take the
course to unedge it all. Sir, I beseech
you, doe not per-plexe her; griefes, alas,
will have a vent: I dare 65 undertake
Madam Hippolita will now freely heare
you. *Soran.* Talke to a woman frantick!
— Are these the fruits of your love?
Hip. They are the fruites of thy untruth,
false man! 70 57 *the.* G-D, thy.
Didst thou not sweare, whil'st yet my
husband liv'd,
That thou wouldst wish no happinesse on earth
More then to call me wife? Didst thou
not vow
When hee should dye to marry mee? —
for which
The devill in my blood, and thy protests,
75
Caus'd mee to counsaile him to un-
dertake
A voyage to Ligorne, for that we heard
His brother there was dead and left a
daughter
Young and unfriended, who, with much
adoe,
I wish't him to bring hither. He did so,
g
And went; and, as thou know'st, dyed

on the way.

Unhappy man, to buy his death so deare,
With my advice! Yet thou, for whom I did it,
Forget' st thy vowes, and leav'st me to my shame.
Soran. Who could help this?
Hip. Who! perjur'd man, thou couldst, g
If thou hadst faith or love.
Soran. You are deceiv'd:
The vowes I made, if you remember well,
Were wicked and unlawfull; 'twere more sinne
To keepe them then to breake them: as for mee
I cannot maske my penitence. Thinke thou 9
How much thou hast digrest from honest shame
In bringing of a gentleman to death
Who was thy husband; such a one as hee,
So noble in his quality, condition,
.,. Learning, behaviour, entertainment, love, 95
As Parma could not shew a braver man.
Vas. You doe not well; this was not your promise. *Soran.* I care not; let her know her mon- struous life.
Ere Fle be servile to so blacke a sinne,
I'le be a curse. Woeman, come here no more; 100
Learne to repent and dye; for, by my honour,
I hate thee and thy lust: you have beene too foule. £'V.
Vas. This part has beene scurvily playd.
Hip. How foolishly this beast contemnes his fate,
And shuns the use of that which I more scornc 105
Then I once lov'd, his love! But let him goe;
My vengeance shall give comfort to his woe.
She offers to goe away. Vas. Mistresse, Mistresse, Madam Hippolita! pray, a word or two.
Hip. With mee, sir? no *Vas.* With you, if you please. *Hip.* What is't? *Vas.* I know you are infinitely mov'd now, and you thinke you have cause: some I confesse

you have, but sure not so much as you imagine. 115 *Hip.* Indeed! *fas.* O you were miserably bitter, which you followed even to the last sillable. Faith, you were somewhat too shrewd; by my life, you could not have tooke my lord in a worse timeizo since I first knew him; to morrow you shall finde him a new man. *Hip.* Well, I shall waite his leasure. *Vas.* Fie, this is not a hearty patience; it 'omes sowerly from you: troth, let me perswade 125 /ou for once. *Hip. aside.* I have it, and it shall be so; thanks, opportunity! — Perswade me to what? *Vas.* Visitt him in some milder temper. O, if you could but master a little yourfemall spleen, 130 how might you winne him! *Hip.* Hee wil never love me. Vasques, thou hast bin a too trusty servant to such a master, and I beleeve thy reward in the end wil fal l out like mine. 135 *Vas.* So, perhaps, too. *Hip.* Resolve thy selfe it will. Had I one so true, so truely honest, so secret to my counsels, as thou hast beene to him and his, I should thinke it a slight acquittance, not onely to make 140 him maister of all I have, but even of my selfe. *Vas.* O, you are a noble gentlewoman. *Hip.* Wu't thou feede alwayes upon hopes? Well, I know thou art wise, and see'st the reward of an old servant daily, what it is. 145 *Vas.* Beggery and neglect. *Hip.* True; but, Vasques, wer't thou mine, and wouldst bee private to me and my designes, I here protest my selfe and all what I can else call myne should be at thy dispose. 150 *Vas. aside.* Worke you that way, old moule? then I have the wind of you. — I were not worthy of it by any desert that could lye— within my compasse; if I could — *Hip.* What then? 155 *Vas,* I should then hope to live in these my old yeares with rest and security. *Hip.* Give me thy hand: now promise but thy silence,
And helpe to bring to passe a plot I have,
And here in sight of heaven, that being done, 160
I make thee lord of mee and mine estate.
Vas. Come, you are merry; this is such a happinesse that I can neither thinke or beleeve.
Hip. Promise thy secresie, and 'tis con-

firm'd. *Vas.* Then here I call our good genii for wit-165 nesses, whatsoever your designes are, or agains j whomsoever, I will not onely be a speciall actc? therein, but never disclose it till it be effected. *Hip.* I take thy word, and, with that, thee for mine; Come, then, let's more conferre of this anon. 15. 165-6 *for witnesses.* So G-D. Q, foe-witnessa. On this delicious bane my thoughts shall banquet;

Revenge shall sweeten what my griefes have tasted. *Exeunt,* SCENA TERTIA.

The street. Enter Richardetto and Philotis. Richardetto. Thou see'st, my lovely neece, these strange mishaps, How all my fortunes turne to my disgrace, Wherein I am but as a looker on Whiles others act my shame, and I am silent.
Pbilotis. But, unkle, wherein can this borrowed shape Give you content?
Rich. I'le tell thee, gentle neece:
Thy wanton aunt in her lascivious riotts
Lives now secure, thinkes I am surely dead
In my late journey to Ligorne for you,—
As I have caus'd it to be rumord out,—
Now would I see with what an impudence
Shee gives scope to her loose adultery,
And how the common voyce allowes hereof:
Thus farre I have prevail'd.
Phil. Alas, I feare
You meane some strange revenge.
Rich. O, be not troubled; i
Your ignorance shall pleade for you in all:
But to our businesse. What! you learnt for certaine
How Signior Florio meanes to give his daughter In marriage to Soranzo?
Phil. Yes, for certaine. *Rich.* But how finde you young Annabella's love M Inclind to him?
Phil. For ought I could perceive,
She neyther fancies him or any else.
Rich. There's mystery in that which time must shew. Shee us'd you kindly?
Phil. Yes. *Rich.* And crav'd your company? *Phil.* Often. *Rich.* 'T is well; it goes as I could wish. » I am the doctor now; and as for you, None knowes you; if all faile not, we shall thrive. *(Enter

Grimaldi.

But who comes here? I know him; 'tis Grimaldi,

A Roman and a souldier, neere allyed

Unto the Duke of Montferrato, one J»

Attending on the nuntio of the pope

14-5 *Shu usd... could wish.* Q does not observe vene arrangement.

That now resides in Parma; by which meanes

He hopes to get the love of Annabella.

Grimaldi. Save you, sir.

Rich. And you, sir. *Gri.* I have heard

Df your approv'd skill, which through the city 35

Is freely talkt of, and would crave your ayd.

Rich, For what, sir? *Gri.* Marry, sir, for this — But I would speake in private.

Rich. Leave us, cozen. *Exit Phi. Gri.* I love faire Annabella, and would know

40 Whether in arts there may not be receipts To move affection. *Rich.* Sir, perhaps there may;

But these will nothing profit you.

Gri. Not mee? *Rich.* Unlesse I be mistooke, you are a man Greatly in favour with the cardinall. 45 *Gri.* What of that?

Rich. In duty to his grace,

I will be bold to tell you, if you seeke

To marry Florio's daughter, you must first

Remove a barre twixt you and her.

?«'. Whose that?

41 *art,.* Changed by D in G-D to *art.*

Rich. Soranzo is the man that hath her heart; And while hee lives, be sure you cannot speed. *Gri.* Soranzo! what, mine enemy! is't hee? *Rich.* Is hee your enemy? *Gri.* The man I hate

Worse then confusion; I'le tell him streight.

Rich. Nay, then, take mine advice, 55

Even for his graces sake, the cardinall:

I 'le finde a time when hee and shee doe meete,

Of which I'le give you notice; and, to be sure

Hee shall not scape you, I'le provide a poyson

To dip your rapiers poynt in: if hee had 60

As many heads as Hidra had, he dyes.

Gri. But shall I trust thee, doctor? *Rich.* Asyourselfe;

Doubt not in ought; thus shall the fates decree,

By me Soranzo falls, that ruin'd mee.

Exeunt. SCENA QUARTA — *Another part of the" street. Enter Donado, Bergetto and Poggio. Donado.* Well, sir, I must bee content to be both your secretary and your messenger my selfe.

I cannot tell what this letter may worke; but, as sure as I am alive, if thou come once to talke with her, I feare them wu't marre whatsoever I *S* make. 54 *ttll.* G suggests *to.* 64 *ruin'd.* So G-D. *Q,* min'd. *Eergetto.* You make, unkle? Why am not I bigge enough to carry mine owne letter, I pray? *Do.* I, I, carry a fooles head o' thy ownel Why, thou dunce, wouldst thou write a letter, 10 and carry it thy selfe? *Ber.* Yes, that I wudd, and reade it to her with my owne mouth; for you must thinke, if shee will not beleeve me my selfe when she hearees me speake, she will not beleeve anothers 15 handwriting. O, you thinke I am a blocke-head, unkle. No, sir. *Poggio knowes I have indited a letter my selfe; so I have. *Poggio.* Yes, truely, sir; I have it my pocket. *Do. A* sweete one, no doubt; pray, let's see't. zo *Ber.* I cannot reade my owne hand very well, Poggio; reade it, Poggio. *Do.* Begin. *Poggio reades. Pog.* Most dainty and honey-sweete Mistresse: J could call you faire, and lie as fast as any that* 15 *loves you; tut my unkle being the elder man, I leave it to him, as more fit for his age and the colour of his beard. I am wise enough to tell you I can board where I see occasion; or if you like my unkles wit better then mine, you shall marry mee; if you like* 3 *mine better then his, I will marry you in spight of your teeth.* &, *commending my best parts to you I rest Tours upwards and downewards, or you may chose,* jj *Bergetto, Ber.* Ah, ha! here's stuffe, unkle! *Do.* Here's stuffe indeed to shame us all. Pray, whose advice did you take in this learned letter? 40 *Pog.* None, upon my word, but mine owne. *Ber.* And mine, unkle, beleeve it, no bodies else 5 'twas mine owne brayne, I thanke a good wit for't. *Do.* Get you home, sir, and looke you keepe 45 within doores till I returne. *Ber.* How! that were a jest indeede; I scorne

it, yfaith. *Do.* What! you doe not? *Ber,* Judge me, but I doe now. *Pog.* Indeede, sir, 'tis very unhealthy. *Do.* Well, sir, if I heare any of your apish running to motions and fopperies till I come backe, you were as good no; looke too't. *Exit Do. Ber.* Poggio, shall's steale to see this horse 55 with the head in's tayle? *Pog.* I, but you must take heede of whipping. *Ber.* Dost take me for a child, Poggio? Come, honest Poggio. *Exeunt.* SCENA QUINTA — *Friar Bonaventura's cell.*

Enter Fryar and Giovanni.

Fryar Peace, thou hast told a tale whose every

word

Threatens eternall slaughter to the soule:

I'me sorry I have heard it; would mine eares

Had beene one minute deafe, before the houre

That thou cam'st to mee! O young man castaway,

By the relligious number of mine order,

I day and night have wak't my aged eyes

Above thy strength, to weepe on thy behalfe;

But Heaven is angry, and be thou resolv'd

Thou art a man remark't to tast a mischiefe. 10

Looke for't; though it come late, it will come

sure.

Giovanni. Father, in this you are uncharitable; What I have done I'le prove both fit and good. It is a principall, which you have taught When I was yet your scholler, that the f rame 15 And composition of the minde doth follow The frame and composition of body: So, where the bodies furniture is beauty, j Themindes must needs bevertue; which allowed, 6 *numher.* G suggests *founder.* 8 *thy.* G, my. 15 *f famt.* Corrected by G. 17 *of hody.* G-D supplies the before *hody.*

Vertue it selfe is reason but refin'd, 20

And love the quintessence of that: this proves

My sisters beauty being rarely faire

Is rarely vertuous; chiefly in her

love,

And chiefely in that love, her love to me.

If hers to me, then so is mine to her;
2

Since in like causes are effects alike.

Fry. O ignorance in knowledge! Long agoe,

How often have I warn'd thee this before!

Indeede, if we were sure there were no deity,

Nor heaven nor hell, then to be lead alone 30

By natures light—as were philosophers

Of elder times — might instance some defence.

But 'tis not so; then, madman, thou wilt fnule

That nature is in heavens positions blind.

Gio. Your age o're rules you; had you youth like mine, 35

You'd make her love your heaven, and her divine.

Fry. Nay, then I see th' art too farre sold to hell:

It lies not in the compasse of my prayers

To call thee backe; yet let me counsell thee:

Perswade thy sister to some marriage. 40

Gio. Marriage! why, that's to dambe her; that's to prove Her greedy of variety of lust. *Fry.* O fearefull! if thou wilt not, give me leave To shrive her, lest shee should dye un-absolv'd.

Gio. At your best leasure, father: then shee'le tell you 45

How dearely shee doth prize mymatchlesse love;

Then you will know what pitty 'twere we two

Should have beene sundred from each others
armes.

View well her face, and in that little round

You may observe a world of variety; 50

For colour, lips; for sweet perfumes, her breath;

For jewels, eyes; for threds of purest gold,

Hayre; for delicious choyce of flowers, cheekes;

Wonder in every portion of that throne.

Heare her but speake, and you will sweare the
sphseres 55

Make musicke to the cittizens in heaven.

But, father, what is else for pleasure fram'd,

Least I offend your eares, shall goe un-nam'd.

Fry. The more I heare, I pitty thee the more,

That one so excellent should give those parts 6

All to a second death. What I can doe

Is but to pray; and yet I could advise thee,

Wouldst thou be rul'd.

Gio. In what?

Fry. Why, leave her yet: 50 *world of variety.* G-D, world's variety.

The throne of mercy is above your trespasse;

Yet time is left you both —

Gio. To embrace each other. 65

Else let all time be strucke quite out of number:

She is like mee, and I like her, resolv'd.

Fry. No more! I'le visit her; this grieves me most, Things being thus, a paire of soules are lost.

Exeunt. SCENA SEXTA. *A room 'in Fiorso's bouse.'*

Enter Florio, Donado, Annabella, Putana.

Florio. Where's Giovanni? *Annabella.* Newly walk't abroad,

And, as I heard him say, gon to the fryar,

His reverent tutor.

Flo. That's a blessed man,

A man made up of holinesse: I hope

Hee'le teach him how to gaine another world. 5

Donado. Faire gentlewoman, here's a lette sent

To you from my young cozen; I dare sweare

He loves you in his soule: would you cou)
heare

Sometimes what I see dayly, sighes and teares,

As if his breast were prison to his heart.
ie

Flo, Receive it, Annabella.

Anna. Alas, good man! *Do.* What's that she said? *'Putana.* And please you, sir, she sayd, " Alas, good man!" Truely I doe commend him to her 'S every night before her first sleepe, because I would have her dreame of him; and shee harkens to that most relligiously. *Do.* Say'st so? Godamercy, Putana, there's something for thee; and prythee doe what thou »o canst on his behalfe; sha' not be lost labour, take my word for't. *Put.* Thanke you most heartily, sir; now I have a feeling of your mind, let mee alone to worke. a5 *Anna.* Guardian! *Put.* Did you call? *Anna.* Keepe this letter. *Do.* Signior Florio, in any case bid her reade it instantly. 30 *Flo.* Keepe it for what? pray, reade it mee here right. *Anna.* I shall, sir. *She reades. Do.* How d'ee finde her inclin'd, signior? *Flo.* Troth, sir, I know not how; not all so well

As I could wish.

Anna. Sir, I am bound to rest your cozens debter. 21 *Sha'* G-D, 'shall. ji *Keepe it for whatt* G-D, Keep it! for what-

The jewell I'le returne; for if he love,

I'le count that love a jewell.

Do. Marke you that? —

Nay, keepe them both, sweete maide.

Anna. You must excuse mee. 4.

Indeed I will not keepe it.

Flo. Where's the ring

That which your mother in her will bequeath'd,

And charg'd you on her blessing not to give't

To any but your husband? Send backe that.

Anna. I have it not.

Flo. Ha! have it not! where is't? 45 *Anna.* My brother in the morning tooke it from me, Said he would weare't to day.

Flo. Well, what doe you say

To young Bergetto's love? Are you content

To match with him? Speake.

Do. There's the poynt, indeed.

Anna aside. What shal I doe? I must say something now. j *Flo.* What say? Why d'ee not speake? *Anna.* Sir, with your leave,

Please you to give me freedome?

Flo. Yes, you have. *Anna.* Signior Donado, if your nephew meane To rayse his better fortunes in his match, 52 *Tes,you have.* G-D supplies "it" after "have." The hope of mee will hinder such a hope:

Sir, if you love him, as I know you doe, 55

Find one more worthy of his choyce then mee.

In short, I'me sure, I sha' not be his wife.

Do. Why, here's plaine dealing; I commend thee for't;

And all the worst I wish thee, is heaven blesse thee!

Your father yet and I will still be friends— 60 Shall we not, Signior P'lorio?

Flo. Yes, why not?

Looke, here your cozen comes.

Enter Bergetto and Poggio. Do. aside. Oh, coxcombe! what doth he make here? *Bergetto.* Where's my unkle, sirs? 65 *Do.* What's the newes now? *Her.* Save you, unkle, save you! You must not thinke I come for nothing, maisters. And how, and how is't? What, you have read my letter? Ah, there I — tickled you, yfaith. 70 *Poggio aside to Ber..* But 'twere better you had tickled her in another place. *Ber.* Sirrah sweet-heart, I'le tell thee a good jest; and riddle what 'tis. *dnna.* You say you'd tell mee. 75 75 *you'd.* G-D, you'll. *Ber.* As I was walking just now in the streete, I mett a swaggering fellow would needs take the wall of me; and because hee did thrust me, I very valiantly cal'd him rogue. Hee hereupon bad me drawe; I told him I had more wit then I so: but when hee saw that I would not, hee did so maule me with the hilts of his rapier that my head sung whil'st my feete caper'd in the ken-nell. *Do.* Was ever the like asse seene? I *Anna.* And what did you all this while? *Ber.* Laugh at him for a gull, till I see the blood runne about mine eares, and then I could not choose but finde in my heart to cry; till a fellow with a broad beard — they say hee is a 9 new-come doctor — cald mee into his house, and gave me a playster; looke you, here 'tis; and, sir, there was a young wench

washt my face and hands most excellently; yfaith, I shall love her as long as I live for't, — did she not, Poggio? *Pog.* Yes, and kist him too. *Ber.* Why, la, now, you thinke I tell a lye, unkle, I warrant. *Do.* Would hee that beate thy blood out of thy head had beaten some wit into it; for I feare ic thou never wilt have any. *Ber.* Oh, unkle, but there was a wench would 87 in. G-D, saw. 91 *i-s.* So GD, Q, this. have done a mans heart good to have lookt on her; by this light, shee had a face mee-thinks worth twenty of you, Mistresse Annabella. j *Do.* Was ever such a foole borne? *Anna.* I am glad shee lik't you, sir. *Ber.* Are you so? By my troth, I thanke you, forsooth. *Flo.* Sure, 'twas the doctors neece, that was no last day with us here. *Ber.* 'Twas shee! 'Twas shee! *Do.* How doe you know that, simplicity? *Ber.* Why doe's not hee say so? If I should have sayd no, I should have given him the lye, 115 unkle, and so have deserv'd a dry beating again: I'le none of that. *Flo.* A very modest welbehav'd young maide As I have seene. *Do.* Is shee indeed? *Flo.* Indeed .Shee is, if I have any judgement. no *Do.* Well, sir, now you are free; you need not care for sending letters. Now you are dis-mist; your mistresse here will none of you. *Ber.* No! why what care I for that? I can have wenches enough in Parma forhalfeacrownens 1 peece — cannot I, Poggio? 118-9 *A very ... ha've scene.* Q prints on one line. 119-20 *Indeed shee ii... judgement.* G-D prints on one line. as here. *Pog.* I'le warrant you, sir. *Do.* Signior Florio,

I thanke you for your free recourse you gave
For my admittance; and to you, faire maide, 1jo
That jewell I will give you 'gainst your marriage.
Come, will you goe, sir?

Ber. I, marry, will I. Mistres, farwell, mis-tres; I'le come againe to morrow— farwell, mistres. *Exit Do., Ber.* £3" *Png.* 135 *Enter Gio. Flo.* Sonne, where have you beene? What, alone, alone, still, still?

I would not have it so; you must forsake This over bookish humour. Well, your

sister
Hath shooke the foole off.

Giovanni. 'Twas no match for her.

Flo. 'Twas not indeed; I ment it nothing lesse; 140

Soranzo is the man I onely like.

Looke on him, Annabella. — Come, 'tis suppertime,

And it growes late. *Exit Florio.*

Gio. Whose jewell's that?

Anna. Some sweet-hearts. *Gio.* So I thinke. 118-32 Q prints as prose. 136-9 *Sonne... off.* Q prints as prose. 136 *still.* G-D omits second *still.* *Anna.* A lusty youth, 145

Signior Donado, gave it me to weare Against my marriage.

Gio. But you shall not weare it;

Send it him backe againe.

Anna. What, you are jealous? *Gio.* That you shall know anon, at better leasure. Welcome sweete night! the evening crownes the day. *Exeunt.* 150 145-8 *A lusty... gave it me.* Q prints as one line; *to wtan... marriage,* the next; *but you.. . agoint,* the next; *What ... jtaloui T,* the last. ACTUS TERTIUS.

SCENA PRIMA. *A room in Donado's house.'*

Enter Bergetto and Poggio. Bergetto. Do'es my unkle thinke to make mee a baby still? No, Poggio, he shall know I have a skonce now. *Poggio.* I, let him not bobbe you off like an ape with an apple. 5 *Ber.* 'Sfoot, I will have the wench, if he were tenne unkles, in despight of his nose, Poggio. *Pog.* Hold him to the grynd-stone, and give not a jot of ground; shee hath in a manner promised you already. 1« *Ber,* True, Poggio, and her unkle, the doctor, swore I should marry her. *Pog.* He swore, I remember. *Ber.* And I will have her, that's more. Did'st see the codpeice-poynt she gave me, and the i box of mermalade? *Pog.* Very well; and kist you, that my chopps watred at the sight on't. There's no way but to clap up a marriage in hugger mugger. *Ber.* I will do't; for I tell thee, Poggio, I « begin to grow valiant, methinkes, and my courage begins to rise. 11-12 *True... her.* Q gives this to Poggio. *Pog.* Should you be afraid of your unkle? *Ber.* Hang him, old doating rascall! no, I say t will have her. »5 *Pog.*

Lose no time, then. *Ber.* I will beget a race of wise men and con-ttables that shall cart whoores at their owne charges; and breake the dukes peace ere I have done my selfe. Come away. *Exeunt.* 30 SCENA SECUNDA. *Aroom in Florio''sbouse. Enter Florio, Giovanni, Soranzo, Annabella, Putana and Vasques.*
Florio. My Lord Soranzo, though I must con- fesse

The proffers that are made me have beene great

In marriage of my daughter, yet the hope

Of your still rising honours have pre-vaild

Above all other joynctures: here shee is; 5

She knowes my minde; speake for your selfe to her.

And heareyou, daughter, see you use him nobly.

For any private speech I'le give you time.

Come, sonne,and you the rest; let them alone;

Agree as they may.

IO *Agra.* G-D inserts a second *they* after agree.
Soranzo. I thanke you, sir. »,,, *Giovanni aside to Annd.* Sister, be not all woeman; thinke on me. *Soran.* Vasques! *Vasques.* My lord. *Soran.* Attend me without. *Exeunt omnes; manet Soran. & Anna. Annabella.* Sir, what's your will with me? *Soran.* Doe you not know What I should tell you?

Anna. Yes, you'le say you love mee. *Soran.* And I'le sweare it too; will you be- leeve it? 15 *Anna.* "Tis not poynt of faith.

Enter Giovanni above.

Soran. Have you not will to love? *Anna.* Not you.

Soran. Whom then?

Anna. That's as the fates inferre. *Gio. aside.* Of those I'me regient now. *Soran.* What meane you, sweete F *Anna.* To live and dye a maide. *Soran.* Oh, that's unfit.

Gio. aside. Here's one can say that's but a womans noate. 20 *Soran.* Did you but see my heart, then would you sweare — 15-14 *Dot... ttll you f* Q prints as one line.. 1 6 *'Tit not.* G-D,'Z«no. *Anna.*

That you were dead! *Gio. aside.* That's true, or somewhat neere it. *Soran.* See you these true loves teares? *Anna.* No. *Gio. aside.* Now shee winkes. *Soran.* They plead to you for grace. *Anna.* Yet nothing speake. *Soran.* Oh, grant my suite. *Anna.* What is't? *Soran.* To let mee live— » *Anna.* Take it. *Soran.* Still yours. *Anna.* That is not mine to give. *Gio. aside.* One such another word would kil his hopes. *Soran.* Mistres, to leave those fruitlesse strifes of wit,

I know I have lov'd you long,and lov'dyou truely:

Not hope of what you have, but what you are, 30

Have drawne me on; then let mee not in vaine

Still feele the rigour of your chast disdaine.

I'me sicke, and sicke to th' heart.

Anna. Helpe! aquavitae!

Soran. What meane you? *Anna.* Why, I thought you had beene sicke. *tg I know.* G-D, omits I. 31 *Have.* G-D, hath.. *Soran.* Doe you mocke my love? *Gio. aside.* There, sir, shee was too nimble. 35 *Soran. aside.* 'Tis plaine; shee laughes at me. — These scornefull taunts Neither become your modesty or yeares. *Anna.* You are no looking-glasse; or if you were, I'de dresse my language by you. *Gio. aside.* I'me confirm'd. *Anna.* To put you out of doubt, my lord, meethinks e

Your common sence should make you under stand

That if I lov'd you, or desir'd your love,

Some way I should have given you better tast:

But since you are a noble man, and one I would not wish should spend his youth in

hopes,

Let mee advise you here to forbeare your suite,

And thinke I wish you well, I tell you this.

Soran. Is't you speake this?

Anna. Yes, I my selfe; yet know, —

Thus farre I give you comfort, — if mine eyes

Could have pickt out a man, amongst all those 50

That sue'd to mee, to make a husband of,

36-47 *'Tis plaint... tell you this.* Q prints as prose. 46 *here.* G-D omits here.

You should have beene that man: let this suffice.

Be noble in your secresie and wise.

Gio. aside. Why, now I see shee loves me.

Anna. One word more.

As ever vertue liv'd within your mind, 55

As ever noble courses were your guide,

As ever you would have me know you lov'd

me,

Let not my father know hereof by you:

If I hereafter finde that I must marry, It shall be you or none.

Soran. I take that promise. 60 *Anna.* Oh, oh, my head!

Soran. What's the matter? not well? *Anna.* Oh, I begin to sicken! *Gio. aside.* Heaven forbid! *Exit from above. Soran.* Helpe, helpe, within there, ho! Looke to your daughter, Signior Florio. 65 *Re-enter Florio, Giovanni, Putana, Flo.* Hold her up; shee sounes. *Gio.* Sister, how d'ee? *Anna.* Sicke, brother, are you there? *Flo.* Convay her to her bed instantly, whil'st I send for a phisitian; quickly, I say. *Putana.* Alas, poore child! 70 *Exeunt; manet Soranzo.* 65 *Luke... Floria.* Q gives this to Giovanni. *Re-eater Vasques. Vas.* My lord. *Soran.* Oh, Vasques, now I doubly am undone Both in my present and my future hopes: Shee plainely told me that shee could not love, And thereupon soone sickned, and I fear 75 Her life's in danger.

Vas. aside. Byr lady, sir, and so is yours, if you knew all.—'Las, sir, I am sorry for that: may bee 'tis but the maides-sicknesse, an over-fluxe of youth; and then, sir, there is no such 80 present remedy as present marriage. But hath shee given you an absolute deniall? *Soran.* She hath and she hath not; I'me full of griefe; But what she sayd I'le tell thee as we goe. *Exeunt.* SCENA TERTIA.

A room in Florio's house.

Enter Giovanni and Putana

Putana. Oh, sir, wee are all undone, quite undone, utterly undone, and sham'd forever! Your sister, oh, your sister! *Giovanni.* What of her? For heavens sake, speake; how do'es she? 5 *Put.* Oh, that ever I was borne to see this v! *Gio.* She is not dead, ha? is shee? *Put.* Dead? no, shee is quicke; 'tis worse, she is with childe. You know what you have xo done; heaven forgive 'ee! 'Tis too late to repent, now heaven helpe us! *Gio.* With child? how dost thou know't? *Put.* How doe I know't! am I at these yeeres ignorant what the meaning's of quames and 15 ivaterpangs be? of changing of colours, quezi-nesse of stomacks, pukings, and another thing that I could name? Doe not, for her and your credits sake, spend the time in asking how, and which way, 'tis so: shee is quick, upon my 10 word: if you let a phisitian see her water, y'are undone. *Gio.* But in what case is shee? *Put.* Prettily amended: 'twas but a fit, which I soone espi'd, and she must looke for often 15 hence-forward. *Gio.* Commend me to her, bid her take no care;
Let not the doctor visit her, I charge you:
Make some excuse till I returne. — Oh, mee!
I have a world of businesse in my head. — 30
Doe not discomfort her.
12 G-D puts the comma after now. Q, as here. 31-3 *Doe not... well.* Arrangement of G-D. Q makes but " ' lints, beginning the second with If my father.
How doe this newes perplex mee! — If my fathe.
Come to her, tell him shee's recover'd well;
Say 'twas but some ill dyet; d'ee heare, woeman?
Looke you to't. 3$
Put. I will sir. *Exeunt.* SCENA QUARTA.
A room in Florio's bouse.'
Enter Florio and Richardetto.
Florio. And how d'ee finde her, sir?
Ricbardetto. Indifferent well;
I see no danger, scarse perceive shee's sicke,
But that shee told mee shee had lately eaten
Mellownes, and, as shee thought, those

disagreed
With her young stomacke.
Flo. Did you give her ought? 5 *Rich.* An easie surfeit water, nothing else.
You neede not doubt her health: I rather thinke
Her sicknesse is a fulnesse of her blood,—
You understand mee?
Flo. I doe; you counsell well;
And once, within these few dayes, will so order't 10 She shall be married ere shee know the time.
Rich. Yet let not hast, sir, make unworthy choice; That were dishonour. *Flo.* Maister Doctor, no;
I will not doe so neither: in plaine words,
My Lord Soranzo is the man I meane. 15 *Rich.* A noble and a vertuous gentleman.
Flo. As any is in Parma. Not farre hence Dwels Father Bonaventure, a grave fryar, Once tutor to my sonne: now at his cell I'le have 'em married. *Rich.* You have plotted wisely, 2o *Flo,* I'le send one straight to speake with him to night.
Rich. Soranzo's wise; he will delay no time. ' *Flo.* It shall be so. *Enter Fryar and Giovanni. Fryar.* Good peace be here and love! *Flo.* Welcome, relligious fryar; you are one That still bring blessing to the place you come to. s *Giovanni.* Sir, with what speed I could, I did my best
To draw this holy man from forth his cell
To visit my sicke sister; that with words
Of ghostly comfort in this time of neede
Hee might absolve her, whether she live or
die. o *Flo.* 'Twas well done, Giovanni; thou herein Hast shewed a Christians care, a brothers love. Come, father, I'le conduct you to her chamber, Ind one thing would intreat you.
Fry. Say on, sir. *Flo.* I have a fathers deare impression, 35
And wish before I fall into my grave
That I might see her married, as 'tis fit:
A word from you, grave man, will winne her
more
Then all our best perswasions.
Fry. Gentle sir,

All this I'le say, that heaven may prosper her. 40 *Exeunt.* SCENA QUINTA.
*A room in Ricbardetto's
house.*
Enter Grimaldi.
Grimaldi. Now if the doctor keepe his word,
Soranzo,
Twenty to one you misse your bride. I know
'Tis an unnoble act, and not becomes
A souldiers vallour; but in termes of love,
Where merite cannot sway, policy must. 5
I am resolv'd; if this phisitian
Play not on both hands, then Soranzo falls.
Enter Ricbardetto.
Ricbardetto. You are come as I could wish;
this very night
Soranzo, 'tis ordain'd, must bee afEed
8-11 *You are... married. Q* prints u proK.
To Annabella, and, for ought I know, 10
Married.
Gri. How! *Rich.* Yet your patience: —
The place, 'tis Fryar Bonaventures cell.
Now I would wish you to bestow this night
In watching thereabouts; 'tis but a night:
If you misse now, to morrow I'le know all. 15
Gri. Have you the poyson?
Ricb. Here, 'tis in this box:
Doubt nothing, this will doe't; in any case,
As you respect your life, be quicke and sure.
Gri. I'le speede him.
Rich. Doe. Away! for 'tis not safe
You should be seene much here. Ever my love! o *Gri.* And mine to you. *Exit Gri. Rich.* So! if this hitt, I'le laugh and hug revenge;
And they that now dreame of a wedding-feast
May chance to mourne the lusty bridegromes
mine.
But to my other businesse. Neice Philotis! 5 *Enter Philotis. Philotis.* Unkle.

Rich. My lovely neece, You have bethought 'ee? *Phi.* Yes, and, as you counsel'd, 12 *Fryar. Q,* Fryars.
Fashion'd my heart to love him, but hee sweares
Hee will to night be married; for he feares 3
His unkle else, if hee should know the drift,
Will hinder all, and call his couze to shrift.
Rich. To night? why, best of all; but let mee see—
I — ha! — yes, — so it shall be; in disguise Wee'le earely to the fryars; I have thought on't. 35 *Enter Bergetto and Poggio. Phi.* Unkle, hee comes.
Rich. Welcome, my worthy couze. *Bergetto.* Lasse, pretty lasse, come busse, lasse! Aha, Poggio! /J/VA. *aside.* There's hope of this yet. You shall have time enough; withdraw a little; Wee must conferre at large. *Ber.* Have you not sweete-meates or dainty devices for me? 40 *Phi.* You shall enough, sweet-heart. *Ber.* Sweet-heart! marke that, Poggio. By my troth, I cannot choose but kisse thee once more for that word " sweet-heart." Poggio, I have a monstrous swelling about my stomacke, 4 whatsoever the matter be. *Poggio.* You shall have phisick for't, sir. *Rich.* Time runs apace. *Ber.* Time's a blockhead. 38 *Thtrfi...yet.* So G-D. 2 gives this to Philotis. *Rich.* Be rul'd: when wee have done what's fitt to doe, 50
Then you may kisse your fill, and bed her too.
Exeunt. SCENA SEXTA. *Annabella'f chamber Enter tbefryar sitting in a chayre; Annabella kneeling and whispering to him; a table before them and wax-lights. She weepes and wrings her hands. Fryar.* I am glad to see this pennance; for, beleeve me,
You have unript a soule so foule and guilty,
As, I must tell you true, I marvaile how The earth hath borne you up: but weepe, weepe
on; These teares may doe you good; weepe faster yet, Whiles I doe read a lecture.
Annabella. Wretched creature! *Fry.* I, you are wretched, miserably wretched,

Almost condemn'd alive. There is a place,—
List, daughter, — in a blacke and hollow vault,
Where day is never seene; there shines no sunne, But flaming horrour of consuming fires, *Enter thtfryar. Q* adds *in Us study;* this is clearly a mistake """ 's corrected in G-D.
A lightlesse suphure, choakt with smoaky foggs
Of an infected darknesse; in this place Dwell many thousand thousand sundry sorts
Of never dying deaths; there damned soules 15
Roare without pitty; there are gluttons fedd
With toades and addars; there is burning oyle
Powr'd downe the drunkards throate; the usurer
Is forc't to supp whole draughts of molten gold;
There is the murtherer for-ever stab'd, 10
Yet can he never dye; there lies the wanton
On racks of burning steele, whiles in his soule
Hee feeles the torment of his raging lust.
Anna. Mercy! Oh, mercy!
Fry. There stands these wretched things Who have dream't out whole yeeres in lawlesse sheets 25
And secret incests, cursing one another; Then you will wish each kisse your brother gave
Had been a daggers poynt; then you shall heare
How hee will cry," Oh, would my wicked sister
Had first beene damn'd, when shee did yeeld to
lust! " — To
But soft, methinkes I see repentance worke New motions in your heart: say, how is't with you?
Anna. Is there no way left to redeeme my miseries? 24 *ttands.* G-D, stand.
Fry. There is, despaire not; heaven is merci- full
And offers grace even now. 'Tis thus agreed: 35

First, for your honours safety that you marry
The Lord Soranzo; next, to save your soule,
Leave off this life, and henceforth live to him.
Anna. Ay mee!
Fry. Sigh not; I know the baytes of sinne Are hard to leave; oh, 'tis a death to doe't: 40 Remember what must come. Are you content? *Anna.* I am. *Fry.* I like it well; wee'le take the time.— Who's neere us there? *Enter Flork, Giovanni. Florio.* Did you call, father? *Fry.* Is Lord Soranzo come? *Flo.* Hee stayes belowe. *Fry.* Have you acquainted him at full? *Flo.* I have, 45
And hee is over-joy'd.
Fry. And so are wee.
Bid him come neere.
Giovanni aside. My sister weeping, ha! I feare this fryars falshood. — I will call him.
Exit. 45-8 / *have... call him. Q* prints as four lines ending with... *over-joy'd. . . neere... falthood... him. Flo.* Daughter, are you resolv'd? *Anna.* Father, I am. *Re-enter Giovanni witV Soranzo and Vasques. Flo.* My Lord Soranzo, here 50 Give mee your hand; for that I give you this.
Soranzo. Lady, say you so too? *Anna.* I doe, and vow
To live with you and yours.
Fry. Timely resolv'd:
My blessing rest on both! More to be done,
You may performe it on the morningsun. 55
Exeunt. SCENA SEPTIMA. *The street before the monastery. Enter Grimaldi with his rapier drawne and a darke- lanthorne. Grimaldi.* 'Tis early night as yet, and yet too soone
To finish such a worke; here I will lye To listen who comes next. *Hee lies downe.*
Enter Bergetto and Philotis disguis'd; and, after, Richardetto and Poggio.
Bergetto. Wee are almost at the place, I hope,
sweet-heart.
Gri. aside. I heare them neere, and heard one say " sweet-heart." 5 'Tis hee; now guide my hand, some angry justice,

Home to his bosome! Now have at you, sir! 52-3 / *doe.., yours ...* JJ prints as one line. *Strikes Ber. and exit. Her.* Oh, helpe, helpe! here's a stich fallen in my gutts. Oh, for a flesh-taylor quickly! — Poggio! 10 *Philotis.* What ayles my love? *Ber.* I am sure I cannot pisse forward and backward, and yet I am wet before and behind. — Lights! lights! ho, lights! *Pbi.* Alas, some villaine here has slaine my love. 15 *Richardetto.* Oh, heaven forbid it! Raise up the next neighbours

Instantly, Poggio, and bring lights. *Exit Poggio.*

How is't, Bergetto? slaine? It cannot be; Are you sure y'are hurt?

Ber. O, my belly seeths like a porridge-pot! 10 Some cold water, I shall boyle over else: my whole body is in a sweat, that you may wring my shirt; feele here—why, Poggio! *Re-enter Poggio with officers and lights andbalberts.*

Poggio. Here. Alas, how doe you?

Rich. Give me a light. What's here? all blood! O, sirs, 25

Signior Donado's nephew now is slaine.

Follow the murtherer with all the haste

Up to the citty; hee cannot be farre hence:

Follow, I beseech you.

18-19 *It cannot... hurt.* Q prints as one line.

Officers. Follow, follow, follow! *Exeunt officers. Rich.* Teare off thy linen, couz, to stop his wounds. 30

Be of good comfort, man.

Ber. Is all this mine owne blood? Nay, then, good-night with me. Poggio, commend me to my unkle, dost heare? Bid him, for my sake, make much of this wench. — Oh! — I am go-35 ing the wrong way sure, my belly akes so. — Oh, farwell, Poggio! —Oh!— Oh! — *Dyes. Phi.* O, hee is dead! *Pog.* How! dead! *Rich.* Hee's dead indeed;

'Tis now to late to weepe: let's have him home,

And with what speed we may finde out the

murtherer. 40 *Peg.* Oh,my maister! my-maister! mymaister!

Exeunt. SCENA OCTAVA. *A room in Hippolita't house.*

Enter Basques and Hippolita.

Hippolita. Betroath'd?

Casques. I saw it.

Hip. And when's the marriage-day?

Vas. Some two dayes hence. *Hip.* Two dayes! Why, man, I would but wish two houres

To send him to his last and lasting sleepe; j

And, Vasques, thou shalt see I'le doe it bravely.

Vas. I doe not doubt your wisedome, nor, I trust, you my secresie; I am infinitely yours. *Hip.* I wilbe thine in spight of my disgrace.— So soone? O wicked man, I durst be sworne 10 Hee'd laugh to see mee weepe. *Vas.* And that's a villanous fault in him. *Hip.* No, let him laugh; I'me arm'd in my resolves. Be thou still true. *Vas.* I should get little by treachery against so 15 hopefull a preferment as I am like to climbe to.

Hip. Even to my bosome, Vasques! Let my youth

Revell in these new pleasures; if wee thrive,

Hee now hath but a paire of dayes to live. *Exeunt.*

SCENA NONA. *The street before the CardinaFs gates. Enter Florio, Don ado, Richardetto, Poggio and Officers. Florio.* 'Tis bootlesse now to shew your selfe a child,

Signior Donado; what is done, is done:

Spend not the time in teares,but seeke for justice.

Richardetto. I must confesse somewhat I was in fault

That had not first acquainted you what love 5

Past twixt him and my neece; but, as I live,

His fortune grieves me as it were mine owne.

Donado. Alas, poore creature! he ment no man harme; That I am sure of.

Flo. I beleeve that too.

But stay, my maisters, are you sure you saw 10 The murtherer passe here?

//'«/ Officer. And it please you, sir, wee are sure wee saw a ruffian with a naked weapon in his hand all bloody get into my Lord Cardinals Graces gate; that wee are sure of; but for 15 feare of his

grace, bless us, we durst goe no further.

Do. Know you what manner of man hee was? *Second Officer.* Yes, sure I know the man; they say a is a souldier; hee that lov'd your 20 daughter, sir, an't please y'ee; 'twas hee for cer-taine. *Flo.* Grimaldi, on my life! *Second' Officer.* I, I, the same. *Rich.* The Cardinall is no-ble; he no doubt Will give true justice.

Do. Knock, some one, at the gate. 25

Poggio. I'le knocke, sir. *Poggio knocks. Servant (within).* What would 'ee? *Flo.* Wee require speech with the Lord Car-dinall

About some present businesse: pray in-forme

His grace that we are here. 30

Enter Cardinal! and Grimaldi. Cardinal. Why, how now, friends! What saw-cy mates are you

That know nor duty nor civillity?

Are we a person fit to be your boast,

Or is our house become your common inne,

To beate our dores at pleasure? What such haste 35

Is yours as that it cannot waite fit times?

Are you the maisters of this common-wealth,

And know no more discretion? Oh, your newes

Is here before you; you have lost a nephew,

Donado, last night by Grimaldi slaine: 40

Is that your businesse? Well, sir, we have knowledge on't;

Let that suffice.

Grimaldi. In presence of your grace,

In thought I never ment Bergetto harme;

But, Florio, you can tell with how much scorne

Soranzo, backt with his confederates, 45

Hath often wrong'd mee; I to be re-veng'd,—

For that I could not win him else to fight,—

Had thought by way of ambush to have kild him,

But was unluckely therein mistooke;

Else hee had felt what late Bergetto did:

And though my fault to him were meerely chance,

Yet humbly I submit me to your grace,
To doe with mee as you please.
Car. Rise up, Grimaldi.

You cittizens of Parma, if you seeke
For justice, know, as nuntio from the
Pope, 55 For this offence I here receive
Grimaldi Into his holinesse protection.
' Hee is no common man, but nobly
borne, Of princes blood, though you, Sir
Florio, Thought him to meane a hus-
band for your daughter. 60

If more you seeke for, you must goe
to Rome,
For hee shall thither: learne more wit,
for shame.
Bury your dead. — Away, Grimaldi;
leave 'em.
Ex. Car. & Gri.
Do. Is this a church-mans voyce? Dwels
justice here?
Flo. Justice is fledd to heaven, and
comes no
neerer. 65

Soranzo! Was't for him? O, impu-
dence!
Had he the face to speake it, and not
blush?
Come, come, Donado, there's no helpe
in this,
When cardinals thinke murder's not
amisse.
Great men may do there wills, we must
obey; 70
But heaven will judge them for't anoth-
er day.
Exeunt. ACTUS QUARTUS.
SCENA PRIMA. *A room in Florio's house.*
'

A banquet. Hoboyes.
*Enter the Fryar, Giovanni, Annabella,
Philotis, Sor-
anzo, Dona Jo, Florio, Ricbardetto, Putana and
Basques.*
Fryar. These holy rights perform'd,
now take
your times
To spend the remnant of the day in
feast:
Such fit repasts are pleasing to the saints
Who are your guests, though not with
mortall
eyes
To be beheld. Long prosper in this
day, 5

You happy couple, to each others
joy!
Soranzo. Father, your prayer is heard;
the hand of goodnesse
Hath beene a sheild for me against my
death;
And, more to blesse me, hath enricht my
life
With this most precious jewell; such a
prize 10
As earth hath not another like to this.
Cheere up, my love; and, gentlemen my
friends,
Rejoyce with mee in mirth: this day
wee'le crowne
With lusty cups to Annabella's health.
Giovanni (aside. Oh, torture! were the
marriage yet undone, 15
Ere I'de endure this sight, to see my
love
Clipt by another, I would dare confu-
sion,
And stand the horrour of ten thousand
deaths.
Vasques. Are you not well, sir?
Gio. Prethee, fellow, wayte;
I neede not thy officious diligence. 20
Florio. Signior Donado, come, you
must forget Your late mishaps, and
drowne your cares in wine.
Soran. Vasques! *Vas.* My lord. *Soran.*
Reach me that weighty bowle.
Here, brother Giovanni, here's to you;
Your turne comes next, though now a
batche-
lour; 25
Here's to your sisters happinesse and
mine!
Gio. I cannot drinke. *Seran.* What! *Gio.*
'Twill indeede offend me. *Annabella.*
Pray, doe not urge him, if hee be not
willing. *Flo.* How now! what noyse is
this? *Vas.* O, sir, I had forgot to tell you;
certaine 30 young maidens of Parma,
in honour to Madam Annabella's mar-
riage, have sent their loves to 29 *11...
. this t* G-D inserts the stage direction
Hautbtyi before this line. 31 *young.* Q,
youg. her in a masque, for which they
humbly crave your patience and silence.
Soran. Wee are much bound to them; so
much the more 35
As it comes unexpected: guide them in.
Hobojes.
Enter Hippolita and Ladies in white

*routes with gar-
lands of willowes.*
Musicke and a Daunce.
Soran. Thanks, lovely virgins! now
might wee
but know
To whom wee have beene beholding for
this
love, We shall acknowledge it.
Hippolita. Yes, you shall know. *Un-
masks.* What thinke you now? *Omnes.*
Hippolita! *Hip.* 'Tis shee; 40
Bee not amaz'd; nor blush young lovely
bride;
I come not to defraud you of your man:
'Tis now no time to reckon up the talke
What Parma long hath rumour'd of us
both:
Let rash report run on; the breath that
vents it 45
35-6 *Wee... in.* Q prints as prose.
38 *this.* So G-D; so copy in British Museum and copy in Boston Public Library. Dyce's copy had *thy;* so copy in
library of the University of Illinois.
Will, like a bubble, breake it selfe at
last.

But now to you, sweet creature; —
lend's your hand; —

Perhaps it hath beene said that I
would claime
Some interest in Soranzo, now your
lord;
What I have right to doe his soule
knowes best: 50
But in my duty to your noble worth,
Sweete Annabella, and my care of you,
Here take, Soranzo, take this hand from
me;
I'le once more joyne what by the holy
Church
Is finish't and allow'd. Have I done
well? jj
Soran. You have too much ingag'd us.
Hip. One thing more,
That you may know my single charity,
Freely I here remit all interest
I ere could clayme, and give you backe
your
vowes;
And to confirm't, — reach me a cup
of wine, — 60
My Lord Soranzo, in this draught I
drinke
Long rest t'ee! — _Aslde to Vasques._

Looke to it, Vasques.

Vas. Fear nothing.

He gives her a poysond cup; she drinks.
Soran. Hippolita, I thanke you, and will pledge This happy union as another life. — 6j

Wine, there!

Vas. You shall have none; neither shall you pledge her.

Hip. How! *Vas.* Know now, mistresse shee devill, your owne mischievous treachery hath kild you; I 70 must not marry you. *Hip.* Villaine! *Omnes.* What's the matter? *Vas.* Foolish woeman, thou art now like a fire-brand that hath kindled others and burnt thy 75 selfe: — *Tropposperar, inganna,* — thy vaine hope hath deceived thee; thou art but dead; if thou hast any grace, pray. *Hip.* Monster! *Vas.* Dye in charity, for shame. This thing g of malice, this woman, had privately corrupted mee with promise of malice, under this politique reconciliation to poyson my lord, whiles shee might laugh at his confusion on his marriage day. I promis'd her faire, but I knew what my reward 85 should have beene, and would willingly have spar'd her life, but that I was acquainted with the danger of her disposition; and now have fitted her a just payment in her owne coyne: there shee is, shee hath yet — and end thy dayes 90 in peace, vild woman; as for life, there's no hope; thinke not on't. *Omnes.* Wonderfull justice! 76 *inganna.* So G-D. Q, niganna. 82 *malice.* Changed in G-D to *marriage. Richardetto.* Heaven, thou art righteous.

Hip. O, 'tis true;

I feele my minute comming. Had that slave 95

Kept promise,—O, my torment,— thou this

houre

Had'st dyed, Soranzo;—heate above hell fire! —

Yet ere I passe away,—cruell,cruell flames,—

Take here my curse amongst you; may thy bed

Of marriage be a racke unto thy heart, i«»

Burne blood and boyle in vengeance — O, my heart,

My flame's intolerable!—maist thou live

To father bastards; may her wombe bring forth

Monsters; and dye together in your sinnes,

Hated, scorn'd and unpittied — Oh! — Oh! Mj

Dyes. Flo. Was e're so vild a creature?

Rich. Here's the end

Of lust and pride.

Anna. It is a fearefull sight. *Soran.* Vasques, I know thee now a trusty servant,

And never will forget thee. — Come, my love,

Wee'le home, and thanke the heavens for this

escape. u

Father and friends, wee must breake up this mirth; It is too sad a feast. *Donado.* Beare hence the body.

Fry. aside to G/o.. Here's an ominous change!

Marke this, my Giovani, and take heed! I feare the event; that marriage seldome's good"5

Where the bride-banquet so begins in blood.

Exeunt. SCENA SECUNDA. *A room in Richardetto 3 house. Enter Ricbardetto and Philotis. Richardetto.* My wretched wife, more wretched in her shame

Then in her wrongs to me, hath paid too soone

The forfeit of her modesty and life.

And I am sure, my neece, though vengeance

hover,

Keeping aloofe yet from Soranzo's fall, 5

Yet hee will fall, and sinke with his owne weight.

I need not — now my heart perswades me so —

To further his confusion; there is one Above begins to worke: for, as I heare, Debate's already twixt his wife and him 10

Thicken and run to head; shee, as 'tis sayd,

Sleightens his love, and he abandons hers:

Much talke I heare. Since things goe thus, my

a *hath.* Q in Boston Public Library misprints a second *hath* following this j the copy at the University of Illinois has only one.

7 *nma.* G-D puts the dash after *now.* Q prints *naio ...»* in parentheses. neece,

In tender love and pitty of your youth, Mycounsell is, that you should free your yeeres 15

From hazard of these woes by flying hence

To faire Cremona, there to vow your soule

In holinesse a holy votaresse:

Leave me to see the end of these extreames.

All humane worldly courses are uneven;

No life is blessed but the way to heaven.

Philotis. Unkle, shall I resolve to be a nun?

Rich. I, gentle neece, and in your hourely

prayers

Remember me, your poore unhappy unkle.

Hie to Cremona now, as fortune leades,,5

Your home your cloyster, your best friends your beades. Your chast and single life shall crowne your birth;

Who dyes a virgine, live a saint on earth.

Phi. Then farwell, world, and worldly thoughts, adeiu! Welcome, chast vowes; myselfe I yeeld to you. 30 *Exeunt.* 18 *live.* G-D, Uves.

SCENA TERTIA. *A chamber in Soranzo's house.*

Enter Soranzo unbrac't, and Annabella dragg'd in.

Soranzo. Come, strumpet, famous whoore!

were every drop

Of blood that runs in thy adulterous veynes

A life, this sword—dost see't?—should in one

blowe

Confound them all. Harlot, rare, notable harlot,

That with thy brazen face maintainst thy sinne, 5

Was there no man in Parma to be bawd

To your loose cunning whoredome else
but I?
Must your hot ytch and plurisie of lust,
The heyday of your luxury, be fedd
Up to a surfeite, and could none but I 10
  Be pickt out to be cloake to your
close tricks,
Your belly-sports? Now I must be the
dad
To all that gallymaufrey that's stuft
In thy corrupted bastard-bearing
wombe!
Say, must ?
dnnabella. Beastly man, why 'tis thy
fate. 15
I sued not to thee j for, but that I thought
Your over-loving lordship would have
runne
Madd on denyall, had yee lent me time,
I would have told 'ee in what case I
was:
But you would needes be doing.
Soran. Whore of whores! 20
  Dar'st thou tell mee this?
Anna. O, yes; why not?
You were deceiv'd in mee; 'twas not for
love
1 chose you, but for honour: yet know
this,
Would you be patient yet, and hide your
shame,
I'de see whether I could love you.
Soran. Excellent queane! 2j
  Why art thou not with child?
Anna. What needs all this,
When 'tis superfluous? I confesse I am.
Soran. Tell mee by whome. *Anna.* Soft,
sir! 'twas not in my bargaine. Yet some-
what, sir, to stay your longing stom-
acke,
I'me content t'acquaint you with: The
man,
The more then man, that got this
sprightly boy, —
For 'tis a boy, that for glory, sir,
Your heyre shalbe a sonne —
Soran. Damnable monster!
Anna. Nay, and you will not heare, I'le
speake no more. *Soran.* Yes, speake,
and speake thy last. *Anna.* A match, a
match! — 35
This noble creature was in every part 28
sir. G-D omits. 30 *I'me.* G-D, I am.
31 *that for glory, sir.* G-D accepts the
correction of Dodslejr, reading *and*

therefore glory, sir.
So angell-like, so glorious, that a woe-
man
Who had not beene but human, as was
I,
Would have kneel'd to him, and have
beg'd for
love. —
  You! why you are not worthy once
to name 40 His name without true wor-
ship, or, indeede, Unlesse you kneel'd,
to heare another name him.
Soran. What was hee cal'd? *Anna.* Wee
are not come to that;
Let it suffice that you shall have the glo-
ry
To father what so brave a father got. 45
  In briefe, had not this chance falne
out as't doth,
I never had beene troubled with a
thought
That you had beene a creature: — but
for
marriage,
I scarce dreame yet of that.
Soran. Tell me his name.
Anna. Alas, alas, there's all! Will you
be-leeve? 50 *Soran.* What? *Anna.* You
shall never know. *Soran.* How! *Anna.*
Never.
If you doe, let mee be curst.
Soran. Not know it, strumpet! I'ie ripp
up thy heart, And finde it there. *Anna.*
Doe, doe! *Soran.* And with my teeth
Teare the prodigious leacher joynt by
joynt. 55 *Anna.* Ha, ha, ha! the man's
merry.
Soran. Do'st thou laugh?
Come, whore, tell mee your lover, or,
by truth
I'le hew thy flesh to shreds; who is't?
*Anna. Che morte _piu dolce che morire
per
amore? (Sings.*
Soran. Thus will I pull thy hayre, and
thus
  I'le drag 60
  Thy lust be-leapred body through the
dust.
Yet tell his name.
*Anna. Morendo in gra zj la dee morire
senza
dolore. (JSings.*
Soran. Dost thou triumph? The treasure
of the earth

Shall not redeeme thee; were there
kneeling kings
Did begge thy life, or angells did come
downe
To plead in teares, yet should not all
prevayle
Against my rage: do'st thou not tremble
yet?
Anna. At what? to dye? No, be a gallant
hang-man;
  I dare thee to the worst: strike, and
strike home. o I leave revenge behind,
and thou shalt feel't.
59 /"'" 2. ?'-3 *graxia-Q,* gratia. 63 *det.*
Q, Lei. These corrections of the Italian
follow G-D. Weber printed the line
thus: *Morendo in gratia Dei morire
atsssa dalore. Soran.* Yet tell mee ere
thou dyest, and tell mee truely, Knowes
thy old father this? *Anna.* No, by my
life. *Soran.* Wilt thou confesse, and I
will spare thy life? *Anna.* My life? I will
not buy my life so deare. 75 *Soran.* I
will not slacke my vengeance.
Enter Vasques.
Vasques. What d'ee meane, sir? *Soran.*
Forbeare, Vasques; such a damned
whore Deserves no pitty. *Vas.* Now the
gods forefend!
And wud you be her executioner, and
kill her in your rage, too? O, 'twere
most un-manlike. So Shee is your wife:
what faults hath beene done by her before she married you, were not against
you. Alas, poore lady, what hath shee
committed which any lady in Italy in the
like case j " would not? Sir, you must be
ruled by your 85 reason, and not by your
fury; that were unhu-mane and beastly.
Soran. Shee shall not live. *Vas.* Come,
shee must. You would have her confesse the authors of her present misfor-
tunes, 90 I warrant 'ee; 'tis an uncon-
scionable demand, and shee should
loose the estimation that I, for my part,
hold of her worth, if shee had done it.
Why, sir, you ought not of all men living to know it. Good sir, bee reconciled.
Alas, good 95 gentlewoman. 79 *wud.* G-
D, would. 90 *authori.* So Q and G. D
changes to *author. Anna.* Pish, doe not
beg for mee; I prize my life
As nothing. If the man will needs bee
madd,
Why let him take it.

Soran. Vasques, hear'st thou this?

Vas. Yes, and commend her for it; in this 100 shee shews the noblenesse of a gallant spirit, and beshrew my heart, but it becomes her rarely. — *Aside to Soran.* Sir, in any case smother your revenge; leave the senting out your wrongs to mee: bee rul'd, as you respect yjour honour, 105 or you marr all. — *Akud.* Sir, if ever my service were of any credit with you, be not so violent in your distractions: you are married now, what a tryumph might the report of this give to other neglected sutors! 'Tis as manlike to beareuo extremities as god-like to forgive. *Soran.* O, Vasques, Vasques, in this peece of flesh, This faithlesse face of hers, had I layd up 104 *tenting out.* G-D, seen ting-out. 105 j *our.* g, hour.

Scene III. ' UMfii pit£ 93..,

The treasure of my heart! — Hadst thou beene «- vertuous, j j. ' vA" s

Faire wicked woeman, not the match-lesse joyesnj *tf.*

Of life it selfe had made mee wish to live

With any saint but thee: deceitfull crea-ture,

How hast thou mock't my hopes, and in the

shame

Of thy lewd wombe even buried mee alive!

I did too dearely love thee. 1»o

Vas. (aside). This is well; follow this temper with some passion: bee briefe and moving; 'tis for the purpose.

Soran. Be witnesse to my words thy soule and thoughts,

And tell mee, didst not thinke that in my heart 125

I did too superstitiously adore thee?

Anna. I must confesse I know you lov'd mee well. *Soran.* And wouldst thou use mee thus? O

Annabella,

Bee thus assur'd, whatsoe're the vil-laine was

That thus hath tempted thee to this dis-grace, 1

Well hee might lust, but never lov'd like mee:

Hee doated on the picture that hung out Upon thy cheekes to please his hu-mourous eye;

121-3 *This is.. . purpose,* p prints as verse. 129 *Bee thus assur d, tuhatsoe're.* G-D, Be thou assur'd, whoe'er.

Not on the part I lov'd, which was thy heart,

And, as I thought, thy vertues.

Anna. O, my lord! 1jj

These words wound deeper then your sword could do.

Vas. Let mee not ever take comfort, but I begin to weepe my selfe, so much I pitty him: why, madam, I knew when his rage was overpast, what it would come to. 1o *Soran.* Forgive mee, Annabella; though thy youth

Hath tempted thee above thy strength to folly,

Yet will not I forget what I should bee, And what I am — a husband; in that name

Is hid devinity: if I doe finde 145

That thou wilt yet be true, here I remit All former faults, and take thee to my bosome.

Vas, By my troth, and that's a poynt of noble charity.

Anna. Sir, on my knees — *Soran.* Rise up, you shall not kneele.

Get you to your chamber; see you make no shew 150

Of alteration; He be with you streight.

My reason tells mee now that *'Tis as common*

To erre in fraslty as to bee a woeman. Goe to your chamber. *Exit Anna.*

Vas. So! this was somewhat to the mat-ter. 155 What doe you thinke of your heaven of happi-nesse now, sir?

Soran. I carry hell about mee; all my blood Is fir'd in swift revenge. *Vas.* That may bee, but know you how, on 60 on whom? AlaSj to marry a great woeman, being made great in the stocke to your hand, is a usuall sport in these dayes; but to know what secret it was that haunted your cunny-berry,— there's the cunning. 165 *Soran.* I'le make her tell her selfe, or— *Vas.* Or what? — You must not doe so; let me yet perswade your sufferance a little while. Goe to her; use her mildly; winne her, if it be possible, to a voluntary, to a weeping tune: for 170 the rest, if all hitt, I will not misse my marke. Pray, sir, goe in. The next news I tell you shall be won-ders. *Soran,* Delay in vengeance gives a heavyer blow. *Exit. Vas.* Ah, sirrah, here's worke for the nonce! 175 I had a suspicion of a bad matter in my head a pretty whiles agoe; but after my madams scurvy lookes here at home, her waspish perversnesse and loud fault-finding, then I remembred the 160 *you. Q,* yoo. 164 *secret.* G-D accepts Dodsley's emendation, ferret. *haunted.* G-D, hunted. proverbe, that " where hens crowe, and cocks 180 hold their peace, there are sorry houses." Sfoot! if the lower parts of a shee-taylors cun-ning can cover such a swelling in the stomacke, I'le never blame a false stich in a shoe whiles I live againe. Up, and up so quicke? and so quickly too? 185 'Twere a fine policy to learne by whom this must be knowne; and I have thought on't — *Enter Putana.*

Here's the way, or none.— What, cry-ing, old mistresse! Alas, alas, I cannot blame 'ee; wee have a lord, heaven helpe us, is so madde as the 190 devill himselfe, the more shame for him.

Putana. O, Vasques, that ever I was borne to see this day! Doth hee use thee so too sometimes, Vasques? *Vas.* Mee? Why hee makes a dogge of mee; 195 but if some were of my minde, I know what wee would doe. As sure as I am an honest man, hee will goe neere to kill my lady with unkind-nesse. Say shee be with-child, is that such a matter for a young woeman of her yeeres to be 200 blam'd for? *Put.* Alas, good heart, it is against her will full sore. *Vas.* I durst be sworne all his madnesse is for 186 *11hom.* G-D prints a colon after this. *Enter Putana. Q* prints after *shame for hirn.* that shee will not confesse whose 'tis, which hee 205 will know; and when he doth know it, I am so well acquainted with his humour, that hee will forget all streight. Well, I could wish shee would in plaine termes tell all, for that's the way, indeed. 11o *Put.* Doe you thinke so? *Vas.* Fo, I know't; provided that hee did not winne her to't by force. Hee was once in a mind that you could tell, and ment to have wrung it out of you; but I somewhat pacified him for 215 that:

yet sure you know a great deale. *Put.* Heaven forgive us all! I know a little, Vasques. *Vas.* Why should you not? Who else should? Upon my conscience, shee loves you dearely, and 220 you would not betray her to any affliction for the world. *Put.* Not for all the world, by my faith and troth, Vasques. *Vas.* 'Twere pitty of your life if you should 5225 but in this you should both releive her present discomforts, pacifie my lord, and gaine your selfe everlasting love and preferment. *Put.* Do'st thinke so, Vasques? *Vas.* Nay, I know't; sure 'twas some and entire friend. *Put.* 'Twas a deare friend indeed; but — *Vas.* But what? Feare not to name him; my life betweene you and danger; faith, I thinke 'twas no base fellow. 235 *Put.* Thou wilt stand betweene mee and harme? *Vas.* Ud's pitty, what else? You shalbe rewarded, too; trust me. *Put.* 'Twas even no worse then her owne4s brother. *Vas.* Her brother Giovanni, I warrant'ee! *Put.* Even hee, Vasques; as brave a gentle men as ever kist faire lady. O, they love most perpetually. 45 *Vas.* A brave gentleman indeed! Why therein I commend her choyce. — *Aside* Better and better. — You are sure 'twas hee? *Put.* Sure; and you shall see hee will not be long from her too. 250 *Vas.* He were to blame if he would: but may I beleeve thee? *Put.* Beleeve mee! Why do'st thinke I am a Turke or a Jew? No, Vasques, I have knowne their dealings too long to belye them now. 5S *Vas.* Where are you? there within, sirs!
Enter Bandetti.
Put. How now! What are these? *Vas.* You shall know presently. — Come, sirs, 156 *Whtre arc you f* So Q. G-D puts the interrogation mark T *there.* take mee this old damnable hagge, gag her instantly, and put out her eyes, quickly, quickly!i6o *Put.* Vasques! Vasques! *Vas.* Gag her, I say; sfoot, d'ee suffer her to prate? What d'ee fumble about? Let mee come to her. I'le helpe your old gums, you toad-bellied bitch! Sirs, carry her closely into the coale-265 house, and put out her eyes instantly; if shee roares, slitt her nose. D'ee heare,bee speedy and sure. *Exeunt Ban. witb Putana.* Why this is excellent and above

expectation! Her owne., brother? O, horrible! to what a height of liberty 270 p in damnation hath the devill trayn'd our age! her brother, well! there's yet but a beginning; I must to my lord, and tutor him better in his ". , „ points of vengeance. Now I see how a smooth-j tale goes beyond a smooth tayle. — But soft! 275 what thing comes next? *Enter Giovanni..*
Giovanni! as I would wish: my beleefe is strengthned; 'tis as firme as winter and summer.
Giovanni. Where's my sister? *Vas.* Troubled with a new sicknes, my lord; 280 she's somewhat ill.! *Gio.* Tooke too much of the flesh, I beleeve. *Fas.* Troth, sir, and you, I thinke, have e'ne hitt it; but my vertuous lady — 268 *Extant Ban.* So G-U. Q has *Exit with Putana Gio.* Where's shee? 285 *Vas.* In her chamber; please you visit her; she is alone. *Gio. gives him money.* Your liberality hath doubly made me your servant, and ever shall, ever. *Exit Gio. Reenter Soranzo.*
Sir, I am made a man; I have plyed my cue 290 with cunning and successe. I beseech you let's be private.
Soran. My ladyes brother's come; now hee'le know all. *Vas.* Let him know't; I have made some of 295 them fast enough. How have you delt with my lady? *Soran.* Gently, as thou hast counsail'd; O, my soule
Runs circular in sorrow for revenge:
But, Vasques, thou shalt know — 300
Vas. Nay, I will know no more; for now comes your turne to know: I would not talke so openly with you. — *Aside* Let my young mais-ter take time enough, and goe at pleasure; hee is sold to death, and the devill shall not ransome 305 him. — Sir, I beseech you, your privacy.
Soran. No conquest can gayne glory of my feare. *Exeunt . Exeunt. p_, exit.* ACTUS QUINTUS. SCENA PRIMA. *The street before Soranzo's house. Enter Annabella above. Annabella.* Pleasures, farwell, and all yee thriftlesse minutes
Wherein false joyes have spun a weary life!
To these my fortunes now I take my leave.

Thou precious Time that swiftly rid'st in poast
Over the world to finish up the race
Of my last fate, here stay thy restlesse course,
And beare to ages that are yet unborne
A wretched, woefull woemans tragedy!
y conscience now stands up against my lust ith dispositions charectred in guilt,
Enter Fryar below.
And tells mee I am lost: now I confesse,
Beauty that cloathes the out-side ofthe-jace
Is cursed if it be not doath'd with grace.
Here like a turtle mew«d up in a cage,
Un-mated, I converse with ayre and walls,
And descant on my vild unhappinesse.
O, Giovanni, that hast had the spoyle
Of thine owne vertues and my modest fame,
1o *dispoiitiont.* G-D, depositions.
Would thou hadst beene lesse subject to those stars That luckelesse raign'd at my nativity! »o 0 would the scourge due to my blacke offence Might passe from thee, that I alone might feele The torment of an uncontrouled flame!
Fryar. aside. What's this I heare? *Anna.* That man, that blessed fryar,
Who joynd in ceremoniall knot my hand 25
To him whose wife I now am, tpld mee oft 1 troad the path to death, and shewed mee how.
But they who sleepe in lethargies of lust Hugge their confusion, making heaven unjust;
And so did I.
Fry, aside. Here's musicke to the soule! j *Anna.* Forgive mee, my good Genius, and this once
Be helpfull to my ends: let some good man
Passe this way, to whose trust I may commit
This paper double lin'd with teares and blood:
Which being granted, here I sadly vow 5
Repentance, and a leaving of that life I long have dyed in.
Fry. Lady, heaven hath heard you,
And hath by providence ordain'd that

I

Should be his minister for your behoofe.
Anna. Ha, what are you?
Fry. Your brothers friend, the Fryar ;
40 Glad in my soule that I have liv'd
to heare This free confession twixt your
peace and you. What would you, or to
whom? Feare not to speake. *Anna.* Is
heaven so bountifull? Then I have found
More favour then I hop'd. Here, holy
man: 45 *Throwes a letter.*
Commend mee to my brother; give him
that,
That letter; bid him read it, and repent.
Tell him that I, imprison'd in my chamber,
Bard of all company, even of my
guardian,—
Who gives me cause of much suspect,— have
time. 50
To blush at what hath past; bidd him
be wise,
And not beleeve the friendship of my
lord:
I feare much more then I can speake:
good
father,
The place is dangerous, and spyes are
busie;
I must breake off— you'le doe't?
Fry. Be sure I will, 55
And fly with speede.— My blessing
ever rest
With thee, my daughter; live to dye
more
blessed! *Exit Fry. Anna.* Thanks to the
heavens, who have pro- long'd my
breath
To this good use! Now I can welcome
death.
Exit. SCENA SECUNDA. *A room in Soranzo's house. Enter Soranza and Vasques.*
Vasques. Am I to be beleev'd now? First
marry a strumpet that cast her selfe
away upon you but to laugh at your
hornes, to feast on your disgrace, riott
in your vexations, cuckold you in your
bride-bed, waste your estate upon pan-
ders s and bawds — *Soranzo.* No more,
I say, no more! *Vas.* A cuckold is a
goodly tame beast, my lord. *Soran.* I am
resolv'd; urge not another word; 10
My thoughts are great, and all as res-
olute

As thunder. In meane time I'le cause
our lady
To decke her selfe in all her bridall
robes,
Kisse her, and fold her gently in my
armes.
Begone, — yet, heare you, are the bandetti ready 15
To waite in ambush?
Vas. Good sir, trouble not your selfe
about other busines then your owne resolution; remember that time lost cannot
be recal'd.
Soran. With all the cunning words thou
canst, invite 20
The states of Parma to my birth-dayes
feast.
Haste to my brother rivall and his father; Entreate them gently, bidd them
not to fayle. Bee speedy and returne.
Vas. Let not your pitty betray you till
my com-ming backe; thinkeupon incest
and cuckoldry. *Soran.* Revenge is all the
ambition I aspire; To that I'le clime or
fall; my blood's on fire. *Exeunt.* SCENA
TERTIA. *A room in Florio's house. Enter
Giovanni. Giovanni.* Busie opinion is an
idle foole That, as a schoole-rod, keepes a child in awe, Frights the unexperi-
enc't temper of the mind: So did it mee,
who, ere my precious sister Was married, thought all tast of love would dye
In such a contract; but I finde no change
Of pleasure in this formall law of sports.
Shee is still one to mee, and every kisse
As sweet and as delicious as the first I
reap't, when yet the priviledge of youth
Intitled her a virgine. O, the glory Of
two united hearts like hers and mine!
Let poaring booke-men dreame of other
worlds; My world and all of happinesse
is here, And I'de not change it for the
best to come: — A life of pleasure is
Elyzeum. *Enter Fryar.*
Father, you enter on the jubile
Of my retyr'd delights; now I can tell
you
The hell you oft have prompted is
nought else
But slavish and fond superstitious feare;
20
And I could prove it too — *Fryar.*
Thy blindnesse slayes thee:
Looke there, 'tis writt to thee. *Gives
the letter. Gio.* From whom?

Fry. Unrip the seales and see. The
blood's yet seething hot that will anon
15 Be frozen harder then congeal'd cor-
rall. Why d'ee change colour, sonne?
Gio. Fore heaven, you make
Some petty devill factor 'twixt my love
And your relligion-masked sorceries.
Where had you this?
Fry. Thy conscience, youth, is sear'd;
30
Else thou wouldst stoope to warning.
Gio. 'Tis her hand,
I know't; and 'tis all written in her
blood.
She writes I know not what. Death? I'le
not
feare
An armed thunder-bolt aym'd at my
heart.
Shee writes wee are discovered — pox
on dreames 3 5
Of lowe faint-hearted cowardise! —dis-
covered?
The devill wee are! which way is't pos-
sible?
Are wee growne traytours to our owne
delights?
Confusion take such dotage! 'tis but
forg'd;
This is your peevish chattering, weake
old man! 40
Enter Vasques.
Now, sir, what newes bring you?
Vasques. My lord, according to his
yearely custome, keeping this day a
feast in honour of his birth-day, by mee
invites you thither. Your worthy father,
with the popes reverend nuntio, 45 and
other magnifico's of Parma, have
promis'd their presence; wil't please
you to be of the number?
Gio. Yes, tell them I dare come. *yas.*
Dare come? 50 *Gio.* So I sayd; and tell
him more, I will come. *Vas.* These
words are strange to mee. *Gio.* Say I
will come. *Vas.* You will not misse? 55
Gio. Yet more! I'le come, sir. Are you
an-swer'd? *Vas.* So Fle say. — My service to you. *Exit 7as. Fry.* You will not
goe, I trust. *Gio.* Not goe? for what?
Fry. O, doe not goe; this feast, Fle gage
my life, *Enter Vasquet.* Q prints this below the question following. 49 *them.*
G—D, him. 56 Q has a semicolon after
come and a comma after *sir.*

Is but a plot to trayne you to your ruine.
60

Be rul'd, you sha' not goe.
Gio. Not goe! stood Death
Threatning his armies of confounding plagues
With hoasts of dangers hot as blazing starrs,
I would be there. Not goe? yes, and re-solve
To strike as deepe in slaughter as they all; 65

For I will goe.
Fry. Go where thou wilt: I see
The wildnesse of thy fate drawes to an end,
To a bad fearefull end. I must not stay
To know thy fall; backe to Bononia I
With speed will haste, and shun this comming
blowe. 70

Parma, farwell; would I have never knowne thee, Or ought of thine! Well, young man, since no prayer

Can make thee safe, I leave thee to despayre.
Exit Fry.
Gi'o. Despaire or tortures of a thousand hells, All's one to mee; I have set up my rest. 75

Now, now, worke serious thoughts on banefull plots;

Be all a man, my soule; let not the curse
Of old prescription rent from mee the gall
Of courage, which inrolls a glorious death.
If I must totter like a well-growne oake, 80
Some under shrubs shall in my weighty fall
Be crusht to splitts; with me they all shall perish!
Exit. SCENA QUARTA. *A hall in Soranzo's house. Enter Soranzo, Vasques and Bandetti. Soranzo.* You will not fayle, or shrinke in the attempt?
Vasques. I will undertake for their parts. — Be sure, my maisters, to be bloody enough, and as unmerciful! ? if you were praying upon a 5 rich booty on the very mountaines of Liguria. For your pardons trust to my lord; but for reward you shall trust none but your owne

pockets. *Bandetti omnes.* Wee'le make a murther. *Soran.* Here's gold; here's more; want nothing. What you do 10 Is noble, and an act of brave revenge. I'le make yee rich, bandetti, and all free. *Omnes.* Liberty! Liberty! *Vas.* Hold; take every man a vizard. When yee are withdrawne, keepe as much silence as 15 you can possibly. You know the watch-word; till which be spoken, move not; but when you heare that, rush in like a stormy flood: I neede not instruct yee in your owne profession. *Omnes.* No, no, no. 2o *Vas.* In, then: your ends are profit and preferment: away! *Exeunt Bandetti. Soran.* The guests will all come, Vasques? *Vets.* Yes, sir. And now let me a little edge your resolution: you see nothing is unready to 15 this great worke, but a great mind in you. Call to your remembrance your disgraces, your losse of honour, Hippolita's blood; and arme your courage in your owne wrongs; so shall you best right those wrongs in vengeance, which you may 30 truely call your owne. *Soran.* 'Tis well: the lesse I speake, the more I burne,
And blood shall quench that flame.
Vas. Now you begin to turne Italian. This 'beside: — when my young incest-monger comes, 35 hee wilbe sharpe set on his old bitt: give him time enough, let him have your chamber and bed at liberty; let my hot hare have law ere he be hunted to his death, that, if it be possible, hee may poast to hell in the very act of his damnation. 40 *Soran.* It shall be so; and see, as wee would wish,
Hee comes himselfe first.
_Enter Giovanni.
Welcome, my much-lov'd brother:
Now I perceive you honour me; y'are welcome.
But where's my father?
22 *Exeunt. Q, Exit. Enter Giovanni. Q prints in somewhat broken type in the margin at the left.*
Giovanni. With the other states,
Attending on the nuntio of the pope, 45
To waite upon him hither. How's my sister?
Soran. Like a good huswife, scarcely ready yet; Y'are best walke to her chamber. *Gio.* If you will. *Soran.* I must

expect my honourable friends; Good brother, get her forth. *Gio.* You are bus-ie, sir. 5 *Exit Giovanni. Vas.* Even as the great devill himselfe would have it! Let him goe and glut himselfe in his owne destruction. Harke, the nuntio is at hand: good sir, be ready to receive him. *Flourisb. Enter Cardinall, Florio, Don-ado, Richardetto, and Attendants. Soran.* Most reverend lord, this grace hath made me proud, 55
That you vouchsafe my house; I ever rest
Your humble servant for this noble favour.
Cardinall. You are our friend, my lord: his

Holinesse
Shall understand how zealously you honour
Saint Peters vicar in his substitute: 60

Our speciall love to you.
Soran. Signiors, to you
My welcome, and my ever best of thanks
For this so memorable courtesie.
Pleaseth your grace to walke neere?
Car. My lord, wee come

To celebrate your feast with civill mirth, 65

As ancient custome teacheth: we will goe.
Soran. Attend his grace there! Signiors, keepe your way. *Exeunt.* SCENA QUIN-TA. *Annabels chamber.' Enter Giovanni and Annabella lying on a bed. Giovan-ni.* What, chang'd so soone! Hath your new sprightly lord Found out a tricke in night-games more then wee
Could know in our simplicity? Ha! is't so?
Or does the fitt come on you to prove treacher-ous
To your past vowes and oathes?
Annabella. Why should you jeast
At my calamity, without all sence
Of the approaching dangers you are in?
Gio. What danger's halfe so great as thy re volt? Thou art a faithlesse sister, else thou know'st Malice or any treachery beside 10 64 *to.* G-D omitt.

Would stoope to my bent browes: why I hold fate

Clasp't in my fist, and could com-

mand the course
Of times eternall motion, hadst thou beene
One thought more steddy then an ebbing sea.
And what? you'le now be honest — that's re-
solv'd? 15 Anna. Brother, deare brother, know what I have beene,

And know that now there's but a dyning time
Twixt us and our confusion: let's not waste
These precious houres in vayne and use-
lesse
speech.

Alas, these gay attyres were not put on 20

But to some end; this suddaine solemne feast
Was not ordayn'd to riott in expence;
I, that have now beene chambred here alone,
Bard of my guardian or of any else,
Am not for nothing at an instant free'd 25

To fresh accesse. Be not deceiv'd, my brother,
This banquet is an harbinger of death
To you and mee; resolve your selfe it is,
And be prepar'd to welcome it.!
17 *dyning time.* G-D, dining-time, which Dyce says is the reading of his quarto. A copy in the British Museum, according to D, gives *dying time.* The copies in the Boston Public Library and the library of the University of Illinois have *dyning. Gia.* Well, then:

The schoole-men teach that all this globe of earth 3
Shalbe consum'd to ashes in a minute.
Anna. So I have read too. *Gio.* But 'twere somewhat strange
To see the waters burne: could I beleeve
This might be true, I could beleeve as well
There might be hell or heaven.
Anna. That's most certaine. 35 *Gio.* A dreame, a dreame! else in this other world Wee should know one another.
Anna. So wee shall. *Gio.* Have you heard so? *Anna.* For certaine. *Gio.* But d'ee thinke
That I shall see you there?—You looke

on mee?
    May wee kisse one another, prate or laugh, 40 Or doe as wee doe here?
Anna. I know not that.
But good, for the present what d'ee meane
To free your selfe from danger? Some way, thinke
How to escape: I'me sure the guests are come.
38-41 *But fee thinke... doe here?* Q breaks this up into sir short lines ending with *thinke... there... mee... another.. . laugh... here.* 42 *good.* G-D, brother, substituted for the sake of the metre.
Gio. Looke up, looke here; what see you in my face? 4 *Anna.* Distraction and a troubled countenance.
Gio. Death and a swift repining wrath: —
yet looke;
What see you in mine eyes?
Anna. Methinkes you weepe. i *Gio.* I doe indeed; these are the funerall teares
Shed on your grave; these furrowed up my cheekes 50
When first I lov'd and knew not how to woe.
Faire Annabella, should I here repeate
The story of my life, wee might loose time.
Be record all the spirits of the ayre
And all things else that are, that day and night, 55
Earely and late, the tribute which my heart
Hath paid to Annabella's sacred love
Hath been these teares, which are her mourners
now!
    Never till now did nature doe her best
To shew a matchlesse beauty to the world, 60
Which in an instant, ere it scarse was seene,
The jealous Destinies require againe.
46 *countenance.* G-D, *conscience,* Dodsley's correction.
51 *To«.* G-D, woo, and so the copy at the University of Illinois. 62 *require.* G-D, requir'd. Dycc sayt in a note that the , Pray, Annabella, pray! Since wee must part, Goe thou, white in thy soule, to fill a throne ' Of innocence and sanctity in heaven. g

Pray, pray, my sister!
Anna. Then I see your drift —
Yee blessed angels, guard mee!
Gio. So say I!
Kisse mee! If ever after times should heare
Of our fast-knit affections, though perhaps
The lawes of conscience and of civil
_use 70
    May justly blame us, yet when they but know
Our loves, that love will wipe away that rigour,
Which would in other incests bee abhorr'd.
Give mee your hand: how sweetely life doth
runne
    In these well-coloured veines! how constantly 7$ These palmes doe promise health! But I could chide
    With nature for this cunning flattery.
Kisse mee againe! — Forgive mee.
Anna. With my heart.
Gio. Farwell! *Anna.* Will you begone?
Gio. Be darke, bright sunne,
And make this mid-day night, that thy guilt rayes go May not behold a deed will turne their splendour quarto has *require;* the quarto at the University of Illinois has
    More sooty then the poets faigne their Stix! — One other kisse, my sister.
Anna. What meanes this? *Gio.* To save thy fame, and kill thee in a kisse. *Stats her.*
Thus dye, and dye by mee, and by my hand! 85
Revenge is mine; honour doth love command.
Anna. Oh, brother, by your hand!
Gio. When thou art dead
    I'le give my reasons for't; for to dispute
With thy—even in thy death — most lovely
beauty
    Would make mee stagger to performe this act 90 Which I most glory in.
Anna. Forgive him, heaven—and me my sinnes! Farwell.
Brother unkind, unkind — mercy, great heaven!
—Oh!— Oh! *Dyes. Gio.* She's dead,

alas, good soule! The hap- lesse fruite
That in her wombe receiv'd its life from mee 95
Hath had from mee a cradle and a grave.
I must not dally. This sad marriage-bed
In all her best bore her alive and dead.
Soranzo, thou hast mist thy ayme in this;
I have prevented now thy reaching plots, 100
And kil'd a love for whose each drop of blood
I would have pawn'd my heart. —
Fayre Annabella,
How over-glorious art thou in thy wounds,
Tryumphing over infamy and hate! —
Shrinke not, couragious hand; stand up, my heart, 105
And boldly act my last and greater part!
Exit with the body, SCENA SEXTA. *A banquetsng room in So-ranzo's bouse. A banquet. Enter Cardinal!, Florio, Don-ado, Soranzo, Richar-detto, Vasques, and attendants; they take their places. Vasques aside to Soran..* Remember, sir, what you have to do; be wise and res-olute.
Soranzo aside to Vas.. Enough: my heart is fix't. — Pleaseth your grace To taste these course confections; though the use Of such set enterteyments more consists 5
In custome then in cause, yet, rev-erend sir,
I am still made your servant by your presence.
Cardinall. And wee your friend.
Soran. But where's my brother Giovanni?
Enter Giovanni with a heart upon his dagger.
Giovanni. Here, here, Soranzo! trim'd in reek-
ing blood 10 That tryumphs over death, proud in the spoyle Of love and vengeance! Fate, or all the powers That guide the motions of immortall soules, Could not prevent mee.
4 *courts.* G-D coarse. 5 *tntertcymtnts,* G-D, entertainment:!. *Car.* What meanes this? 15 *Florio.* Sonne Giovanni! *Soran.* aside. Shall I be forestall'd? *Gio.* Be not amaz'd: if your misgiving hearts Shrinke at an idle sight, what

bloodlesse feare Of coward passion would have ceaz'd your sences, ao Had you beheld the rape of life and beauty Which I have acted! — My sis-ter, oh, my sister!
Flo. Ha! What of her? *Gio.* The glory of my deed
Darkned the mid-day sunne, made noone as night.
You came to feast, my lords, with dainty fare: 25
I came to feast too, but I dig'd for food In a much richer myne then gold or stone
Of any value ballanc't; 'tis a heart,
A heart, my lords, in which is mine in-tomb'd.
Looke well upon't; d'ee know't? 30
Vas. What strange ridle's this?
Gio. 'Tis Annabella's heart, 'tis; why d'ee startle? I vow 'tis hers; this daggers poynt plow'd up
Her fruitefull wombe, and left to rnee the fame
Of a most glorious executioner. 35
Flo. Why, mad-man, art thy selfe?
Gio. Yes, father, and that times to come may know
How as my fate I honoured my revenge, List, father, to your eares I will yeeld up How much I have deserv'd to bee your sonne. 40
Flo. What is't thou say'st?
Gio. Nine moones have had their changes Since I first throughly view'd and truely lov'd Your daughter and my sister. *Flo.* How! alas, my lords,
Hee's a frantick mad-man!
Gio. Father, no.
For nine moneths space in secret I en-joy'd 45
Sweete Annabella's sheetes; nine mon-eths I liv'd
A happy monarch of her heart and her. —
Soranzo, thou knows't this: thy paler cheeke
Beares the confounding print of thy dis-grace;
For her too fruitfull wombe too soone bewray'd 50
The happy passage of our stolne de-lights,
And made her mother to a child un-borne.

Car. Incestuous villaine!
Flo. Oh, his rage belyes him. *Gio.* It does not; 'tis the oracle of truth; I vow it is so. 43-4 *Hoio!... mad-man! Q* prints as one line. *Soran.* I shall burst with fury. — 55
Bring the strumpet forth!
Vas. I shall, sir. *Exit Pas. Gio.* Doe, sir. — Have you all no faith
To credit yet my triumphs? Here I sweare
By all that you call sacred, by the love I bore my Annabella whil'st she liv'd, 60
These hands have from her bosome ript this heart.
Enter Vas. Is't true, or no, sir?
Vas. 'Tis most strangely true. *Flo.* Cursed man! — have I liv'd to — *Dyes.*
Car. Hold up Florio!
Monster of children, see what thou hast done — Broake thy old fathers heart. — Is none of you 65 Dares venter on him?
Gio. Let'em! Oh, my father,
How well his death becomes him in his griefes!
Why this was done with courage. Now survives
None of our house but I, guilt in the blood
Of a fayre sister and a haplesse father. 7o
Soran. Inhumane scorne of men, hast thou a thought T'out live thy murthers?
Gio. Yes, I tell thee, yes: 63 *Holdup Fhrio.* G-D puts a comma before Florio. For in my fists I beare the twists of life. Soranzo, see this heart which was thy wives;
Thus I exchange it royally for thine, *Stats bim. 7$*
And thus, and thus! Now brave revenge is mine.
Soranzo falls.
Vas. I cannot hold any longer; you, sir, are you growne insolent in your butcheries? Have at you! *Figbt. Gio.* Come, I am arm'd to meete thee. 80 *Vas.* No! will it not be yet? If this will not, another shall. Not yet? I shall fitt you anon. — *Vengeance! Enter Banditti.*
Gio. Welcome! come more of you; what e're
you be,
I dare your worst — *They surround and*

stab him. 85
Oh, I can stand no longer! Feeble armes
Have you so soone lost strength? *Falls.*
'
Vas. Now you are welcome, sir! —
Away, my maisters, all is done; shift for
your selves, your reward is your owne;
shift for your selves. 90 *Banditti.* Away,
away! *Exeunt Banditti. Vas.* How d'ee,
my lord? See you this?
Pointing to Gio.
How is't?
Soran. Dead; but in death well pleased
that
I have liv'd
77 *you. Q* lias no punctuation after *you.*
To see my wrongs reveng'd on that
blacke devill. 95
 O, Vasques, to thy bosome let mee
give
My last of breath; let not that lecher
live. —
Oh! — *Dyes.*
Vas. The reward of peace and rest be
with him, my ever dearest lord and
maister! 100 *Gio.* Whose hand gave
mee this wound?
Vas. Mine, sir; I was your first man:
have you
enough?
Gio. I thanke thee; thou hast done for
me But what I would have else done on
my selfe. Ar't sure thy lord is dead? *Vas.*
Oh, impudent slave, 105
As sure as I am sure to see thee dye!
Car. Thinke on thy life and end, and
call for mercy. *Gio.* Mercy? why I have
found it in this justice.
Car. Strive yet to cry to heaven.
Gio. Oh, I bleed fast!
Death, thou art a guest long look't for; I
embrace 110 Thee and thy wounds. Oh,
my last minute comes!
 Where e're I goe, let mee enjoy this
grace, Freely to view my Annabella's
face. *Dyes. Donado.* Strange miracle of
justice!
Car. Rayse up the citty; wee shall be
murdered all! 115 *Vas.* You neede not
feare, you shall not; this strange taske
being ended, I have paid the duty to
the sonne which I have vowed to the
father. *Car.* Speake, wretched villaine,
what incarnate feind Hath led thee on to
this? 11o *Vas.* Honesty, and pitty of my

maisters wrongs: for know, my lord, I
am by birth a ᴊSpaniard, brought forth
my countrey in my youth by Lord Soranzo's father, whom whil'st he lived
I serv'd faithfully; since whose death
I12$ have beene to this man as I was to
him. What I have done was duty, and
I repent nothing, but that the losse of
my life had not ransom'd his. *Car.* Say,
fellow, know'st thou any yet un- natn'd
Of counsell in this incest? 130 *Vas.* Yes,
an old woeman, sometimes guardian to
this murthered lady. *Car.* And what's
become of her? *Vas.* Within this roome
shee is; whose eyes, after her confession, I caus'd to be put out, but 135 kept
alive to confirme what from Giovanni's
owne mouth you have heard. Now, my
lord, what I have done you may judge
of, and let your owne wisedome bee a
judge in your owne reason. *Car.* Peace!
— First this woeman, chiefe in these effects, 140
My sentence is, that forthwith shee be
tane
Out of the citty, for examples sake,
There to be burnt to ashes.
Do. 'Tis most just.
Car. Be it your charge, Donado, see it
done. *Do.* I shall. 145 *Vas.* What for
mee? If death, 'tis welcome: I have
beene honest to the sonne as I was to the
father. *Car.* Fellow, for thee, since what
thou did'st was done
Not for thy selfe, being no Italian, 150
 Wee banish thee for ever; to depart
Within three dayes: in this wee doe dis-
pense
With grounds of reason, not of thine offence.
Vas. 'Tis well: this conquest is mine,
and I rejoyce that a Spaniard out-went
an Italian in 155 revenge. *Exit Vas. Car.*
Take up these slaughtered bodies, see
them buried;
 And all the gold and jewells, or whatsoever,
Confiscate by the canons of the church,
We ceaze upon to the popes proper use.
160
Richardetto discovers himself. Your
graces pardon: thus long I liv'd disguis'd
 To see the effect of pride and lust at
once

Brought both to shamefull ends.
Car. What! Richardetto, whom wee
thought for dead?
Do. Sir, was it you — *Rich.* Your friend.
Car. Wee shall have time 165
To talke at large of all; but never yet
Incest and murther have so strangely
met.
Of one so young, so rich in natures
store,
Who could not say, ' *Tis pitty shee's a
whoore?*
Exeunt. FINIS.

 The generall commendation deserved
by the actors in their presentment of this
tragedy may easily excuse such few
faults as are escaped in the printing. A
common charity may allow him the
ability of spelling, whom a secure confidence assures that hee cannot ignorantly
erre in the application of sence.
to ' *For tht meaning of angle woreh see
the Glossary.* 3. John, Earle of Peterborough. This nobleman was in favour
with both James I and Charles I. He
was created Earl of Peterborough by letters patent of March 9, 1627-8. See article in *Dictionary of National Biogra-
phy* on Henry Mordaunt, second Earl of
Peterborough. 3. first fruites of my leasure. This might refer to the termination
of some piece of legal business or even
to permanent retirement from the legal
profession; but, as Gilford says, " so little of Ford's personal history is known,
that no allusion to any circumstance peculiar to himself can be explained." 7,
49. Bononia. The Latin form of
Bologna, the seat of the oldest university in Europe. 9, s. stand to your tackling. Defend yourself. 9, 8-9. Wilt thou
to this geere? Do you wish to fight? n,
50. I should have worm'd you. Gifford
says,
' The allusion is to the practice of cut-
ting what is called the *worm from* under
a dog's tongue, as a *preventive of* madness." Of. "Some of our preachmen are
grown dog mad, there's a worm got into
their tongues as well as their heads.''
Familiar Letters of Jama llmoell, II, p.
197, Boston, 1907.
11, 50-51. for running madde. For fear
of your running mad. 12, 62. unspleen'd
dove. According to popular belief, the

dove owed its gentle disposition to its lack of gall. Sir Thomas Browne exposed this vulgar error" in *Pseudodoxia Epidemica,* Bk. sn, Chap. 3. 14, 125-6. an elder brother... coxcomb. Fleay thought these words contained "a personal allusion to Richard Perkins as having acted those parts for the King's Men, and now personating Bergetto for the Queen's." The suggestion is closely associated with hit contention that the play was produced about 1626, which has not met with approval. 30, 56. Padua. The seat of the famous university founded in the thirteenth century, and in the sixteenth and seventeenth centuries particularly flourishing. Coryat tells us that he was conducted about the city by " two English gentlemen that were then commorant in Padua when I was there, Mr. Moore Doctor of Hhysicke, and Mr. Willoughby a learned Student in the University." *Cruditiet,* vol. s, p. 299, Glasgow, 1905. 31, 5. Sanazar. Jacopo Sannazaro was born at Naples in 1458, and died in the same city in 1530. Th» work of his which exerted the widest influence in England was his prose romance, the *Arcadia.* 32, 13. his briefe Encomium. Clifford quotes a line and a half of this poem, which may be found in *Coryat's Crudities,* vol. 1, page 302, Glasgow, 1905:

Viderat Adrians Venetam Neptunus in undst

Stare urbem, & toto ponere jura man: Nunc mibi Tarpeias, quantumvis Juppiter, arces

Objice, & ilia tui moenia Martis, ait. Si pelago Tybrim praefero, urbem aopice utramque,

Illam homines dscae, bane posuissc Deot.

Coryat says that he heard the poet had a " hundred crownes bettowed upon him," and that he wishes his friend "Mr. Benjamin Johnson were so well rewarded." It is perhaps worth noting that James Howell sends this hexastich with an English translation in a letter to Robert Brown of the Middle Temple from Venice, August 1*1,* 1621. The editions of 1645 and 1650 as wellas Miss Repplier's recent edition *(Familiar Letters,* 1907) differ in several points from

Coryat's version. Howell says: " Sannazaro had given him by Saint Mark a hundred zecchins for every one of these verses, which amounts to 300 pounds. " Since Ford, as well as Brown, was a member of the Middle Temple, it is of some interest also that Howell announces the sending of a " parcel of Italian books" requested by Brown.
33, 30. foyle to thy unsated change. Must I serve as a dull *background* to give the zest of contrast to your lust? 36, 107. his woe. The" woe occasioned by his falsehood." G. 39, 5. this borrowed shape. His disguise at physician. 39, 13. common voyce allows hereof. What people in general think of this matter. 41, 4i-z. Whether in arts... to move affection.

An inquiry as to the value of love-potions, charms, etc.
42, 52. Soranzo 1 what, mine enemy 1 Gifford notes this passage as a case of forgetfulness on Ford's part: " It is strange that this should appear a new discovery to Grimaldi, when he had been fully apprised of it in the rencontre with Vasques in the first act." As a matter of fact, the information that Soranzo has the father's word and the daughter's heart is given by Florio just after Grimaldi leaves the stage. Grimaldi had reason to know that Soranzo was his rival, but not that he was the accepted lover. 45, 15-17. the frame and composition... body.

Cf. " The temperature of the mind follows the temperature of the body; which certain axiom — says that sage prince of philosophers, Aristotle—is evermore infallible." *Honour Triumphant s Worhs of John Ford* nI, 359. 69, 8-25. There is a place... lawlesse sheets. 92, 103-4. smother your revenge. On the ethics and

There seem to be some reminiscences here of *Pierce Ptnnilesa:* " A place of horror, stench, and darknesse, where men see meat but can get none, or are ever thirstie, and readie to swelt for drinke, yet have not the power to taste the coole streames that runne hard at their feet... he that all his life time was a great fornicator, hath all the diseases of lust continually hanging upon him... at

so of the rest, as the usurer to swallow moulten gold, the glutton to eate nothing but toades, and the Murtherer to bee still stabd with daggers, but never die." *Worhs of Thomas Nashe,* vol. I, p. 218, London, 1904.
71,39. Ay mee I "The Italian *aime."* Dyce. 83, 76. Troppo Sperar, inganna. *Excessive hope is deceitful.* 83, 90. shee hath yet. There is apparently some defect in the quarto here. 90, 59. Che morte piu dolce che morire per amore? *What death more siveet than to die for love f* 90, 63. morendo in grazia dee morire senza dolore. *To die in grace ? of God is to die without grief.* legality of deferred revenge in seventeenth-century Italy see the pleadings of the lawyers in *The Old Tcllna Baot* (Publication No. 89 of the Carnegie Institution of Washington) edited by Charles W. Hodell, 1908. 95,179-' i-I remembred the proverb that "where hens... sorry houses." Under the date Feb. 5, 1625, Howell writes: " I remember a French proverb *La maijen lt mi'irablt et midiante Oil la foule flat haut qut le toy thante.*

That bouse doth every day more wretched grow

Where the hen louder than the cock doth crow." *Familiar Lattr s tf James Unatll,* vol. I, p. Jol.
108, 75. I have set up my rest. I have made up my mind. no, 38. let my hot hare have law. By the rules of port a hunted animal was allowed a certain time to get the start of his pursuers. 122, 83. Vengeance. The cue for the appearance of the banditti agreed upon in Scene IV of this act.

'Bwrtien f eait THE TEXT

The present edition follows the quarto of 1633, which i s printed with rather more care than the quarto ' *Ti1 Pity* — especially in respect to the arrangement of the lines. As in the case of ' *Tis Pity,* Dyce noticed some slight variations in the copies which he examined, but nothing of significance. There is no evidence of a second edition of the quarto. The old copy has been compared with the texts of Weber and of Gifford and Dyce. The treatment of this text i s identical with that described in the note on ' *Tit Pity.* BROKEN HE ART.

A Tragedy.

By the K i N G's Majefties Seruaftts at the priuate Houfe in the Black.fmep.s.

rideHonor. be fold at Ms Shop, were tbe CUff/s ia *i* tf a a-

SOURCES

Thf.re *u* a hint in the prologue that this play was based on fact, but critics have been obliged to agree with Ward that the "origin of the story on which it is founded *u* unknown.'' (*A History of English Dramatic Literature,* vol. in, page 79.) In the *Publication! of the Modern Language Association of America* xxiv, 2, pp. 274-85, I have attempted to show that the story Ford had in mind was the affair of Sidney and Penelope Devereux, who was married to Lord Rich and later to Mountjoy, Earl of Devonshire. Hartley Coleridge is the only writer that I know of who has pointed in this direction. In a note at the bottom of page xlv in his introduction to the works of Massinger and Ford he says: " Ford no doubt remembered Mountjoy and his hapless love when he wrote the *Broken Heart."* This casual suggestion — unknown to me when I worked out my own theory — rightly, I think, connects Lady Rich with the play; but the circumstances attending her earlier love affair tally much better with the situation laid down in the *Broken Heart.* TO

THE MOST WORTHY DESERVER

OF

THE NOBLEST TITLES IN HONOUR,

WILLIAM, LORD CRAVEN, BARON OF HAMSTEED-MARSHALL

My Lord:

The glory of a great name, acquired by a greater glory of action, hath in all ages liv'd the truest chronicle to his owne memory. In the practise of which argument, your grouth to perfection, even in youth, hath appear' d so sincere, so un-flattering a penne-man, that posterity 5 cannot with more delight read the merit of noble endeavours then noble endeavours merit thankes from posterity to be read with delight. Many nations, many eyes have beene witnesses of your deserts, and lov' d them: be

pleas' d, then, with the freedome of your own nature to admit *one* 10 amongst all particularly into the list of such as honour a faire example of nobilitie. There is a kinde of humble ambition, not un-commendable, when the silence of study breakes forth into discourse, coveting rather encouragement then applause; yet herein censure commonly is too 15 severe an auditor, without the moderation of an able patronage. I have ever beene slow in courtship of greatnesse, not ignorant of such defects as are frequent to opinion; but *Nature.* G-D, name — apparently a mistake. the justice of your inclination to industry emboldens my weaknesse of confidence to rellish an experience of your *20* mercy, as many brave dangers have tasted of your courage. Your lordship strove to be knowne to the world, when the world knew you least, by voluntary but excellent attempts: like allowance I plead of being knowne to your lordship, —in this low presumption, — by tendring to a 25 favourable entertainment a devotion offred from a heart that can be as truely sensible of any least respect as ever professe the owner in my best, my readiest services, a lover of your naturall love to vertue, *John Ford.*

The Sceane.

SPARTA

The speakers names fitted to the qualities.

Amyclas, *common to the kings of Laconia.*

Ithocles, *Honour of Lowelinesse,* a favourite.

Orgilus, *Angry,* sonne to Crotolon.

Bass An Es, *fixation,* a jealous nobleman.

Armostes, *an Appeaser,* a counsellor of state.

Crotolon, *Noyse,* another counsellor.

Prophilus, *Deare,* friend to Ithocles.

Nearchus, *Toung Prince,* Prince of Argos.

Tecnicus, *Artist,* a philosopher.

gUTEMOPHiL, *Glutton*)

Roneas, *Ta,vernbaunter* ' Amelus, *Trusty,* friend to Nearchus. Phulas, *Watchfull,* servant to Bassanes.

Calantha, *Flo-iver of Beauty,* the Kings daughter. Penthea, *Complaint,*

sister to Ithocles. Euphranea, *Joy,* a maid of honour.

Christalla, *Christall).,,,* — *,,.* maids of honour.

Philema, *a Kisse*)

Grausis, *Old Beldam,* overseer of Penthea.

Persons included. Thrasus, *Fiercenesse,* father of Ithocles. Aplotes, *Simplicity,* Orgilus so disguis'd.

Courtiers, Officers, Attendants, &c.

Hmofkil. Q. Lemophil. Craas''j. Q. Grande. *Courtiert... &.* Supplied by G-D. THE PROLOGUE. *Our scaene is Sparta. He whose best of art*

Hath drawne this peece cals it The Broken

Heart.

The title lends no expectation here

Of apish laughter, or of some lame jeere

At place or persons; no pretended clause 5

Of jest's Jit for a brothell courts' applause

From vulgar admiration: such low songs,

Tund to unchast eares, suit not modest tongues.

The virgine sisters then deserv'd fresh bayes

When innocence and sweetnesse crown'd their layes: 10

Then vices gasp'd for breath, whose whole commerce

Was whip'd to exile by unblushing verse.

This law we keepe in our presentment now,

Not to take freedome more then we allow;

What may be here thought a fiction, when times

youth 15 Wanted some riper yeares, was knowne a truth:

In which, if words have cloath'd the subject right,

You may pertake a pitty with delight.

ACTUS PRIMUS SCAENA PRIMA. *A room in Cretelon's bouse. Enter Crotohn and Orgilus.* Crotolon. Dally not further; I will know the reason That speeds thee to this journey. *Orgilus.* Reason? good sir,

I can yeeld many.

Crot. Give me one, a good one;

Such I expect, and ere we part must have:
Athens? pray why to Athens? You intend not 5
To kicke against the world, turne Cynic, Stoicke,
Or read the logicke lecture, or become
An Areopagite, and judge in causes
Touching the common-wealth? For, as I take it,
The budding of your chin cannot prognosticate 10
So grave an honour.
Org. All this I acknowledge.
Grot. You doe! then, son, if books and love of knowledge 4 ere. Q, e're.
Ehflame you to this travell, here in Sparta
You may as freely study.
Org. 'Tis not that, sir.
Crot. Not that, sir? As a father I command thee 15 To acquaint me with the truth. Org. Thus I obey 'ee:
After so many quarrels as dissention,
Fury, and rage had broach't in blood, and sometimes
    With death to such confederates as sided
With now dead Thrasus and your selfe, my lord, 20
Our present king, Amiclas, reconcil'd
Your eager swords, and seal'd a gentle peace:
Friends you profest your selves, which to confirme,
    A resolution for a lasting league
Betwixt your families was entertain'd 5
    By joyning in a Hymenean bond
Me and the faire Penthea, onely daughter
To Thrasus.
Crot. What of this?
Org. Much, much, deere sir.
A freedome of converse, an enterchange
Of holy and chast love, so fixt our soules 30
    In a firme grouth of union, that no time
Can eat into the pledge: we had enjoy'd
The sweets our vowes expected, had not cruelty
Prevented all those triumphs we prepar'd for
By Thrasus his untimely death.

18 *hroach't*. Q, brauch't; G-D, broach'd. 31 *of union*. Q, *of* holy union; but some copies of *Q* omit *holy*. See Dyce's note, *tforks of John Ford*, vol. I, p. 218.

Crot. Most certaine. 35 Org. From this time sprouted up that poyson- ous stalke
Of aconite whose ripened fruit hath ravisht
All health, all comfort of a happy life.
For Ithocles, her brother, proud of youth,
And prouder in his power, nourisht closely 4o
    The memory of former discontents,
To glory in revenge. By cunning partly,
Partly by threats, 'a wooes at once, and forces
His virtuous sister to admit a marriage
With Basanes, a nobleman, in honour 45
    And riches, I confesse, beyond my fortunes.
Grot. All this is no sound reason to importune My leave for thy departure.
Org. Now it followes.
Beauteous Penthea, wedded to this torture
By an insulting brother, being secretly 50
    Compeld to yeeld her virgine freedome up
To him who never can usurpe her heart,
Before contracted mine, is now so yoak'd
To a most barbarous thraldome, misery,
Affliction, that he savors not humanity, 55
    Whose sorrow melts not into more then pitty
In hearing but her name.
Crot. As how, pray?
Org. Bassanes,
The man that calls her wife, considers truly
What heaven of perfection he is lord of
By thinking faire Penthea his: this thought 50
    Begets a kinde of monster-love, which love
Is nurse unto a feare so strong and servile
As brands all dotage with a jealousie.
All eyes who gaze upon that shrine of beauty

He doth resolve doe homage to the miracle; 65
Some one, he is assur'd, may now or then,
If opportunity but sort, prevaile:
So much out of a selfe-unworthinesse
His feares transport him; not that he findes
cause In her obedience, but his owne distrust. 70 Crot. You spin out your discourse.
Org. My griefs are violente:
For knowing how the maid was heretofore
Courted by me, his jealousies grow wild
That I should steale again into her favours,
And undermine her vertues; which the gods 75
Know I nor dare nor dreame of. Hence, from
hence
    I undertake a voluntary exile.
First, by my absence to take off the cares
Of jealous Bassanes; but chiefly, sir,
To free Penthea from a hell on earth; go
Lastly, to lose the memory of something
Her presence makes to live in me afresh.
Grot.   Enough, my Orgilus, enough.
To Athens
I give a full consent. — Alas, good lady! —
Wee shall heare from thee often?
Org. Often.
Crot. See, 85
Thy sister comes to give a farewell.
Enter Euphrania.
Euphranea. Brother!
Org. Euphrania, thus upon thy cheekes I print
A brothers kisse; more carefull of thine honour, Thy health, and thy well-doing, then my life. Before we part, in presence of our father, 90
    I must preferre a suit to 'ee.
Eupbr. You may stile it,
My brother, a command.
Org. That you will promise
To passe never to any man, how ever Worthy, your faith, till, with our fathers leave,
I give a free consent.
Crot. An easie motion! 95

I'le promise for her, Orgilus.
Org. Your pardon;
Euphrania's oath must yeeld me satis-
faction.
93 *To passe never.* G-D, Never to pass.
94 *Worthy.* Q prints at end of preceding
line. *Euphr.* By Vesta's sacred fires I
sweare. *Crot.* And I,
By great Apollo's beames, joyne in the
vow,
Not without thy allowance to bestow
her 100
  On any living.
Org. Deere Euphrania,
Mistake me not: farre, farre 'tis from
my thought,
  As farre from any wish of mine, to
hinder
Preferment to an honourable bed
Or fitting fortune; thou art young and
handsome; 105
And 'twere injustice, — more, a tyran-
nie,—
Not to advance thy merit. Trust me, sis-
ter,
It shall be my first care to see thee
match'd
As may become thy choyce, and our
contents:
I have your oath.
Euphr. You have: but meane you, broth-
er, 110
  To leave us as you say?
Crot. I, I, Euphrania:
He has just grounds direct him. I will
prove
A father and a brother to thee.
Euphr. Heaven
  Does looke into the secrets of all
hearts:
Gods, you have mercy with 'ee, else —
Crot. Doubt nothing; 115
  Thy brother will returne in safety to
us.
Org. Soules sunke in sorrowes never are
without 'em;
They change fresh ayres, but beare their
griefes about 'em. *Exeunt omnes.*
SCAENE 2. *A room in the palace. Flour-
ish. Enter Amyclas the King, Armostes,
Pro-pbilus, and attendants. Amyclas.*
The Spartane gods are gracious; our hu-
mility
  Shall bend before their altars, and
perfume

Their temples with abundant sacrifice.
See, lords, Amyclas, your old King, is
entring
Into his youth againe! I shall shake off 5
  This silver badge of age, and change
this snow
For haires as gay as are Apollo's lockes;
Our heart leaps in new vigour.
Armostes. May old time
  Run backe to double your long life,
great sir!
Amy. It will, it must, Armostes: thy bold
nephew, 10
Death-braving Ithocles, brings to our
gates
Triumphs and peace upon his conquer-
ing sword.
Laconia is a monarchy at length;
Hath in this latter warre trod underfoot.
Messenes pride; Messene bowes her
necke 15
  To Lacedemons royalty. O, 'twas
  A glorious victory, and doth deserve
More then a chronicle; a temple, lords,
A temple to the name of Ithocles!
Where didst thou leave him, Prophilus?
Prophilus. At Pephon, 20
  Most gracious soveraigne; twenty of
the noblest
Of the Messenians there attend your
pleasure
For such conditions as you shall pro-
pose,
In setling peace, and liberty of life.
Amy. When comes your friend the gen-
eral?
Proph. He promis'd 25
To follow with all speed convenient.
*Enter Crotolon, Calantha, Cbrystalla,
Pbilema and
Eufbrania.*
Amy. Our daughter! — Deere Calantha,
the happy newes,
  The conquest of Messene, hath al-
ready
Enrich'd thy knowledge.
Calantha. With the circumstance
  And manner of the fight, related
faithfully 30
  By Prophilus himselfe; but, pray, sir,
tell me,
How doth the youthfull generall de-
meane
His actions in these fortunes?
Proph. Excellent princesse,

  Your owne faire eyes may soone re-
port a truth
Unto your judgement, with what moder-
ation, 35
Calmenesse of nature, measure, bounds
and limits
Of thankefulnesse and joy, 'a doth di-
gest
  Such amplitude of his successe as
would
In others, moulded of a spirit lesse
cleare,
Advance 'em to comparison with heav-
en. 40
  But Ithocles — *Cal.* Your friend —
Proph. He is so, madam,
  In which the period of my fate con-
sists:
He in this firmament of honour, stands
Like a starre fixt, not mov'd with any
thunder
Of popular applause or sudden lightning
45
  Of selfe-opinion. He hath serv'd his
country,
And thinks 'twas but his duty.
Crot. You describe
  A miracle of man.
Amy. Such, Crotolon,
On forfeit of a kings word, thou wilt
finde him.
Harke, warning of his comming! all at-
tend him. 50
*Flourish. Enter Ithocles, Hemophill,
and Groneas;
the rest of the lords ushering him in.*
Amy. Returne into these armes, thy
home, thy sanctuary,
  Delight of Sparta, treasure of my bo-
some,
Mine owne, owne Ithocles!
Ithocles. Your humblest subject.
Armo. Proud of the blood I claime an in-
terest in
As brother to thy mother, I embrace
thee 55
  Right noble nephew.
Itho. Sir, your love's too partial!. *Crot.*
Our country speakes by me, who by thy
valour,
Wisdome, and service, shares in this
great action;
Returning thee, in part of thy due mer-
its,
A generall welcom.

Itho. You exceed in bounty. 60 *Cal.*
Chrystalla, Philena, the chaplet! —
Itho- cles,

Upon the wings of fame the singular
And chosen fortune of an high attempt
Is borne so past the view of common
sight,
That I my selfe with mine owne hands
have
wrought, 65

To crowne thy temples, this provin-
ciall garland;
Accept, weare, and enjoy it, as our gift
Deserv'd, not purchas'd.
Itho. Y'are a royall mayd.
Amy. Shee is in all our daughter. *Itha.*
Let me blush,
Acknowledging how poorely I have
serv'd, 70

What nothings I have done, cotnpar'd
with th' honours

Heap'd on the issue of a willing
minde;
In that lay mine ability, that onely.
For who is he so sluggish from his birth,
So little worthy of a name or country,

That owes not out of gratitude for
life,

Scene nj Eljp ıBroken Jeart 149

A debt of service, in what kinde so-
ever
Safety or counsaile of the common-
wealth
Requires for paiment?
Cal. 'A speaks truth.
Itho. Whom heaven
Is pleas'd to stile victorious, there to
such go

Applause runs madding, like the
drunken priests
In Bacchus sacrifices, without reason
Voycing the leader-on a demi-god:
When as, indeed, each common
souldiers blood
Drops downe as current coyne in that
hard purchase 85
As his whose much more delicate con-
dition
Hath suckt the milke of ease. Judgement
commands,

But resolution executes: I use not,
Before this royall presence, these fit
sleights
As in contempt of such as can direct: 90
My speech hath other end: not to at-
tribute
All praise to one mans fortune, which is
strengthed
By many hands.—For instance, here is
Pro-
philus,

A gentleman — I cannot flatter truth
—
Of much desert; and, though in other
ranke, 95
Both Hemophil and Groneas were not
missing
To wish their countries peace; for, in a
word,
79 '*A.* Here, as elsewhere, G-D prints
He.

All there did strive their best, and 't
was our duty.
Amy. Courtiers turne souldiers? —We
vouchsafe our hand: Observe your great
example. *Hemophil.* With all diligence.
100 *Groneas.* Obsequiously and hourely. *Amy.* Some repose
After these toyles is needfull; we must
thinke on

Conditions for the conquered; they
expect 'em.
On, — come my Ithocles.
Euphr. " Sir, with your favour,
I need not a supporter.
Proph. Fate instructs me. 105 *Exeunt.*
Manent Hemophill, Groneas,
Christalla et Philema.
Hemophill stayes Chrystalla; Groneas,
Philema. Christalla. With me? *Pbilema.*
Indeed I dare not stay. *Hem.* Sweet lady,
Souldiers are blunt, — your lip.
Chris. Fye, this is rudenesse;
You went not hence such creatures.
Gron. Spirit of valour
Is of a mounting nature.
Phil. It appeares so: loa *it. Q,* are.
Pray, in earnest, how many men apeece
no
Have you two beene the death of?
Gron. Faith, not many;
We were compos'd of mercy.
Hem. For our daring
You heard the generals approbation
Before the king.
Chris. You wish'd your countries
peace:
That shew'd your charity; where are
your
spoyles, 115

Such as the souldier fights for?
Phil. They are comming. *Chris.* By the
next carrier, are they not? *Gron.* Sweet
Philena,
When I was in the thickest of mine ene-
mies,
Slashing off one mans head, anothers
nose,
Anothers armes and legs —
Phil. And altogether. no *Gron.* Then
would I with a sigh remember thee,
And cry, " Deare Philena, 'tis for thy
sake
I doe these deeds of wonder!"—dost not
love me
With all thy heart now?
Phil. Now as heretofore.
I have not put my love to use; the
principall 115 Will hardly yeeld an in-
terest.
no *Pray, in earnest, ho.w.* G-D, In
earnest, pray, how. G, Pray now in
earnest, how. *Gron.* By Mars,
I'le marry thee!
Phil. By Vulcan, y'are forsworne,
Except my mind doe alter strangely.
Gron. One word. *Chris.* You lye beyond
all modesty,— for-beare me. *Hem.* I'le
make thee mistresse of a city;
'tis 1o
Mine owne by conquest.
Chris. By petition; sue for't *In forma*
pauperis. —City! kennell. — Gallants!
Off with your feathers, put on aprons,
gallants;
Learne to reele, thrum, or trim a ladies
dog,
And be good quiet soules of peace, hob-
goblins!1s5
Hem. Christalla! *Chris.* Practise to drill
hogs, in hope
To share in the acorns. Souldiers! Corn-
cutters,
But not so valiant; they oft-times draw
blood,
Which you durst never doe. When you
have
practis'd
More wit, or more civility, wee '11
ranke 'ee 140 I'th list of men: till then,
brave things at armes, Dare not to
speake to us, — most potent Groneas
— *Phil.* And Hemophill the hardy,—at
your services.
133 *feathcn. Q,* fathers; G-D, feathera.

Gron. They scorne us as they did before we went. *Hem.* Hang 'em, let us scorne them and be reveng'd. *Exeunt Cbri. et Pbilema.* 145 *Gron.* Shall we?

Hem. We will; and when we sleight them thus,
Instead of following them, they'll follow us.
It is a womans nature.
Gron. 'Tis a scurvy one.
Exeunt omnes. SCENE 3. *The gardens of the palace. A grove Enter Tecnicus a philosopher, and Orgilus disguised like a scholler of bis.*
Tecnicus. Tempt not the stars, young man,
thou canst not play
With the severity of fate: this change
Of habit and disguise in outward view,
Hides not the secrets of thy soule within thee,
From their quicke-piercing eyes, which dive at
all times 5
Downe to thy thoughts: in thy aspect I note
A consequence of danger.
Orgilus. Give me leave,
Grave Tecnicus, without fore-dooming destiny,
Under thy roofe to ease my silent griefes
By applying to my hidden wounds the balme 10
Of thy oraculous lectures: if my fortune
Run such a crooked by-way as to wrest
My steps to ruine, yet thy learned precepts
Shall call me backe, and set my footings streight:
I will not court the world.
Teen. Ah, Orgilus, 15
Neglects in young men of delights and life
Run often to extremities; they care not
For harmes to others who contemne their owne.
Org. But I, most learned artist, am not so much
At ods with nature that I grutch the thrift 1o
Of any true deserver; nor doth malice
Of present hopes so checke them with despaire,

As that I yeeld to thought of more affliction
Then what is incident to frailty: wherefore
Impute not this retired course of living »j
Some little time to any other cause
Then what I justly render: the information
Of an unsetled minde; as the effect
Must clearely witnesse.
Teen. Spirit of truth inspire thee!
On these conditions I conceale thy change, jo
And willingly admit thee for an auditor.
I'le to my study.
Org. I to contemplations:
In these delightfull walkes. *Exit. Tec-nJ—*
Thus metamorphiz'd,
I may without suspition hearken after
Pentheas usage and Euphranias faith. 35
Love! Thou art full of mystery: the deities
Themselves are not secure in searching out
The secrets of those flames which hidden wast
A breast made tributary to the lawes
Of beauty. Physicke yet hath never found 40
A remedy to cure a lovers wound.
Ha! who are those that crosse yon private walke
Into the shadowing grove in amorous foldings?
Propbilus passe th over, supporting Eupbrania, and whispering.
My sister! O, my sister! 'tis Euphrania
With Prophilus: supported too; I would
It were an apparition! Prophilus
Is Ithocles his friend; it strangely pusles me.
Againe! Helpe me, my booke; this schollers habit
Must stand my privilege: my mind is busie; 50
Mine eyes and eares are open.
Walke by, reading.
Enter againe Propbilus and Eupbrania.
Prophilus. Doe not wast 50
The span of this stolne time, lent by the gods For precious use, in nicenesse!

Bright Euphra- nea,
Should I repeat old vowes, or study new,
For purchase of beleefe to my desires —
Org. aside". Desires?
Proph. My service, my integrity — 55
Org. aside. That's better. *Proph.* I should but repeat a lesson
Oft conn'd without a prompter but thine eyes:
My love is honourable —
Org. aside. So was mine
To my Penthea: chastly honourable.
Proph. Nor wants there more addition to my wish 60
Of happinesse then having thee a wife;
Already sure of Ithocles, a friend
Firme and un-alterable.
Org. aside. But a brother
More cruell then the grave.
Euphranea. What can you looke for
In answer to your noble protestations, 65
From an unskilfull mayd, but language suited
To a divided minde?
Org. aside. Hold out, Euphranea!
Euphr. Know, Prophilus, I never under-valued,
From the first time you mentioned worthy love,
Your merit, meanes, or person. It had beene 7
A fault of judgement in me, and a dulnesse
In my affections, not to weigh and thanke
My better starres that offered me the grace
Of so much blisfulnesse. For, to speake truth,
The law of my desires kept equall pace 75
With yours, nor have I left that resolution j
But onely, in a word, what-ever choyce
Lives nearest in my heart must first procure
Consent both from my father and my brother,
E're he can owne me his.
Org. aside. She is forsworne else. So
Proph. Leave me that taske.
Euphr. My brother, e're he parted
To Athens, had my oath.

Org. aside, Yes, yes, 'a had sure. *Propb.*
I doubt not, with the meanes the court
supplies, But to prevaile at pleasure.
Org. aside, Very likely! *Propb.* Meane
time, best, dearest, I may build my
hopes 85
On the foundation of thy constant suf-
france
In any opposition.
Euphr. Death shall sooner
 Divorce life and the joyes I have in
living
Then my chast vowes from truth.
Proph. On thy faire hand
 I seale the like.
Org. aside. There is no faith in
woman— 90 Passion, O, be contain'd!
my very heart-strings Are on the tenters.
Euphr. Sir, we are over-heard, 92 *Sir.* G-
D omits; see note in vol. I, p. 232.
Cupid protect us! 'twas a stirring, sir,
Of some one neere.
Proph. Your feares are needlesse, lady;
 None have accesse into these private
pleasures 95
Except some neere in court, or bosome
student
From Tecnicus his oratory, granted
By speciall.favour lately from the king
Unto the grkve philosopher.
Eupbr. Me thinkes
 I heare one talking to himselfe: I see
him. 100 *Proph.* 'Tis a poore scholler,
as I told you, lady.
Org. asidi. I am discovered. — *As if
think-
ing aloud.* Say it: is it possible
With a smooth tongue, a leering counte-
nance,
Flattery, or force of reason — I come
t'ee, sir—
To turne or to appease the raging sea?
105
Answer to that. — Your art! what art?
to catch
And hold fast in a net the sunnes small
atomes?
No, no; they'll out, they'll out: ye may
as easily
Out run a cloud driven by a northerne
blast,
As fiddle faddle so! Peace, or speake
sense. no
Eupbr. Call you this thing a scholler?
'las hee's lunaticke.

Proph. Observe him, sweet; 'tis but his
recreation.
Org. But will you heare a little! You are
so teatchy,
You keepe no rule in argument. Philos-
ophy
Workes not upon impossibilities, nj
 But naturall conclusions. — Mew! —
absurd I
The metaphysicks are but speculations
Of the celestiall bodies, or such acci-
dents
As not mixt perfectly, in the ayre ingen-
dred,
Appeare to us unnaturall; that's all. no
 Prove it; — yet, with a reverence to
your gravity,
I'le baulke illiterate sawcinesse, submit-
ting
My sole opinion to the touch of writers.
Proph. Now let us fall in with him.
Org. Ha, ha, ha!
 These apish boyes, when they but tast
the grammates 1x5
 And principals of theory, imagine
They can oppose their teachers. Confi-
dence
Leads many into errors.
Proph. By your leave, sir.
Euphr. Are you a scholler, friend?
Org. I am, gay creature,
With pardon of your deities, a
mushrome 130
 On whom the dew of heaven drops
now and then; The sunne shines on me
too, I thanke his beames! Sometime I
feele their warmth; and eat, and sleepe.
Proph. Does Tecnicus read to thee?
Org. Yes, forsooth,
 He is my master surely; yonder dore
 Opens upon his study.
Proph. Happy creatures!
Such people toyle not, sweet, in heats of
state,
Nor sinke in thawes of greatnesse: their
affections
 Keepe order with the limits of their
modesty;
Their love is love of vertue. — What's
thy
name? *Org.* Aplotes, sumptuous master,
a poore wretch.
Euphr. Dost thou want any thing?
Org. Books, Venus, books.
Proph. Lady, a new conceit comes in

my thought,
And most availeable for both our com-
forts.
Euphr. My lord,—
Proph. Whiles I endevour to deserve
145
 Your fathers blessing to our loves,
this scholler
May daily at some certaine houres attend,
What notice I can write of my successe,
Here in this grove, and give it to your
hands:
The like from you tome: so can we never, 150
Barr'd of our mutuall speech, want sure
intelligence;
 And thus our hearts may talke when
our tongues cannot.
Euphr. Occasion is most favourable; use
it.
Proph. Aplotes, wilt thou wait us twice
a day, At nine i' th morning and at foure
at night, 155 Here in this bower, to convey such letters As each shall send to
other? Doe it willingly, Safely, and secretly, and I will furnish Thy study, or
what else thou canst desire. *Org.* Jove,
make me thankfull, thankfull, I beseech
thee, 160
Propitious Jove! I will prove sure and
trusty:
You will not faile me bookes?
Proph. , Nor ought besides
 Thy heart can wish. This ladies
name's Eu- phranea, Mine Prophilus.
Org. I have a pretty memory:
It must prove my best friend. — I will
not misse 165 One minute of the houres
appointed.
Propb.. Write
The bookes thou wouldst have brought
thee in a note, Or take thy selfe some
money.
Org. No, no money:
Money to schollers is a spirit invisible,
We dare not ringer it; or bookes, or
nothing. i
Propb. Bookes of what sort thou wilt:
doe not forget Our names.
Org. I warrant 'ee, I warrant 'ee.
Proph. Smile, Hymen, on the grouth of
our
desires;
Wee'll feed thy torches with eternall

fires!

Exeunt, manet Org. Org. Put out thy torches, Hymen, or their light 175
Shall meet a darkenesse of eternall night.
Inspire me, Mercury, with swift deceits;
Ingenious fate has lept into mine armes,
Beyond the compasse of my braine. — Mortality
   Creeps on the dung of earth, and cannot reach 180
The riddles which are purpos'd by the gods.
Great arts best write themselves in their owne
stories;
   They dye too basely who out-live their glories.

Exit. ACTUS SECUNDUS: SCAENA PRIMA.
.A room in Bassanes' bouse.
Enter Bassanes and Pbulas.

Bassanes. I'le have that window next the
street dam'd up;
It gives too full a prospect to temptation,
And courts a gazers glances: there's a lust
Committed by the eye, that sweats and travels,
Plots, wakes, contrives, till the deformed bear-
whelpe 5
   Adultery be lick'd into the act,
The very act: that light shall be dam'd up;
D'ee heare, sir?

Phulas. I doe heare, my lord; a mason
   Shall be provided suddenly.

Bass. Some rogue,
Some rogue of your confederacy,— factor i
   For slaves and strumpets, — to convey close packets
From this spruce springall and the tother youngster;
   That gawdy eare-wrig, or my lord your patron,
Whose pensioner you are. — I'le teare thy throat
out, Sonne of a cat, ill-looking hounds-head; rip up 15
   Thy ulcerous maw, if I but scent a paper,
A scroll, but halfe as big as what can cover

A wart upon thy nose, a spot, a pimple,
Directed to my lady: it may prove
A mysticall preparative to lewdnesse. 2o

Pbul. Care shall be had. — I will turne every thread About me to an eye. —
Aside Here 's a sweet life! *Bass.* The city houswives, cunning in the traffique
   Of chamber-merchandise, set all at price
By whole-sale; yet they wipe their mouthes, and
simper, 25
   Cull, kisse, and cry " Sweet-hart," and stroake the head Which they have branch'd; and all is well againe!
   Dull clods of dirt, who dare not feele the rubs
Stucke on the fore-heads?

Phul. 'Tis a villanous world,
   One cannot hold his owne in't.
Bass. Dames at court, 30
Who flaunt in riots, runne another byas:
Their pleasure heaves the patient asse that suffers
   Up on the stilts of office, titles, incomes;
Promotion justifies the shame, and sues for't.
   Poore honour! thou art stab'd and bleed'st to death 35
   By such unlawfull hire. The country mistresse
Is yet more wary, and in blushes hides
What ever trespasse drawes her troth to guilt;
But all are false. On this truth I am bold,
No woman but can fall, and doth, or would — 40
Now for the newest newes about the citie;
What blab the voyces, sirrha?

Phul. O, my lord,
   The rarest, quaintest, strangest, tickling newes
That ever —

Bass. Hey da! up and ride me, rascall! What is 't?

Phul. Forsooth, they say, the king has mew'd 45 All his gray beard, instead of which is budded Another of a pure carnation colour, Speckled with greene and russet.

Bass. Ignorant blocke! *Phul.* Yes truly;

and 'tis talkt about the streets,
That since Lord Ithocles came home, the lyons 50
Never left roaring, at which noyse the beares
Have danc'd their very hearts out.

Bass. Dance out thine too.

Pbul. Besides, Lord Orgilus is fled to Athens
Upon a fiery dragon, and'tis thought
A' never can returne.

Bass. Grant it, Apollo! 55 *Phul.* Moreover, please your lordship, 'tis reported
For certaine, that who ever is found jealous
Without apparant proofe that's wife is wanton
Shall be divorc'd: but this is but shenewes;
I had it from a midwife. I have more yet. 60

Bass. Anticke, no more! Ideots and stupid fooles
   Grate my calamities. Why to be faire
Should yeeld presumption of a faulty soule?
Looke to the doores.

Phul. aside. The home of plenty crest him.

Exit Pbul. Bass. Swormes of confusion huddle in my thoughts 65
In rare distemper. Beauty! O, it is
An unmatcht blessing or a horrid curse.

Enter Pentbea and Grausis, an old lady.
Shee comes, she comes! so shoots the morning
forth,
   Spangled with pearles of transparent dew.
The way to poverty is to be rich; 70
   As I in her am wealthy, but for her
In all contents a bankrupt. — Lov'd Penthea!
How fares my hearts best joy?

Grausis. Insooth, not well,
   She is so over-sad.

Bass. Leave chattering, mag-pye. —
Thy brother is return'd, sweet, safe and hon- our'd 75
   With a triumphant victory; thou shalt visit him:
We will to court, where, if it be thy pleasure,
Thou shalt appeare in such a ravishing lustre

Of jewels above value, that the dames
Who brave it there, in rage to be out-
shin'd, 80
Shall hide them in their closets, and un-
seene
Fret in their teares; whiles every won-
dring eye
Shall crave none other brightnesse but
thy presence.
     Choose thine owne recreations; be a
queene
Of what delights thou fanciest best,
what company, 85
What place, what times; doe any thing,
doe all
things
Youth can command; so thou wilt chase
these
clouds
     From the pure firmament of thy faire
lookes.
Grau. Now 'tis well said, my lord.
What,
lady! laugh,
Be merry; time is precious.
Bass. Furies whip thee! *Penthea.* Alas,
my lord, this language to your handmaid
     Sounds as would musicke to the
deafe; I need
No braveries nor cost of art to draw
     The whitenesse of my name into of-
fence;
     Let such, if any such there are, who
covet 95
     A curiosity of admiration,
     By laying out their plenty to full
view,
     Appeare in gawdy out-sides; my at-
tires
     Shall suit the inward fashion of my
minde;
     From which, if your opinion nobly
plac'd, ioo
     Change not the livory your words be-
stow,
     My fortunes with my hopes are at the
highest.
Bass. This house, me thinkes, stands
somewhat too much inward, It is too
melancholy; wee' 11 remove Nearer the
court: or what thinks my Penthea 105
Of the delightfull island we command f
Rule me as thou canst wish. *Pen.* I am
no mistresse;

Whither you please, I must attend; all
wayes
Are alike pleasant to me.
Grau. Island! prison;
     A prison is as gaysome: wee'll no is-
lands: no
     Marry, out upon 'em! whom shall we
see there?
Sea-guls and porpiseis and water-rats
And crabs and mewes and dogfish!
goodly geere
For a young ladies dealing, or an old
ones!
On no termes islands; I'le be stew'd
first.
Bass. aside to Grau.. Grausis,"5
     You are a jugling bawd. — This sad-
nesse, sweetest,
     Becomes not youthfull blood. —
Aside to Grau.
     Tle have you pounded. — for my
sake put on a more chearefull mirth;
Thou't marre thy cheekes, and make me
old in griefes. — *Aside to Grau*
Damnable bitch-foxe!
Grau. I am thicke of hearing 120
Still, when the wind blowes southerly.
What thinke'ee,
     If your fresh lady breed young bones,
my lord?
Wood not a chopping boy d'ee good at
heart?
But, as you said —
Bass, aside to Grau.. Tle spit thee on a
stake, Or chop thee into collops!
Grau. Pray, speake louder. 125
Sure, sure, the wind blowes south still.
Pen. Thou prat'st madly. *Bass.* 'Tis
very hot; I sweat extreamely. —
Now?
Re-Enter Pbulas.
Phul. A heard of lords, sir.
Bass. Ha?
Pbul. A flock of ladies. *Bass.* Where?
Phul. Shoalds of horses. *Bass.* Peasant,
how? *Phul.* Caroches
In drifts — th' one enter, th' other stand
without, sir. 130
And now I vanish. *Exit Pbulas.*
*Enter Propbilus, Hemopbil, Groneas,
Cbristalla and*
Pbilena. Prophilus. Noble Bassanes!
Bass. Most welcome Prophilus, ladies,
gentlemen;
To all my heart is open; you all honour

me, —
Ande. A tympany swels in my head al-
ready, —
Honour me bountifully. — *Aside.* How
they
flutter, 135
     Wagtailes and jayes together!
Proph. From your brother,
By virtue of your love to him, I require
Your instant presence, fairest.
Pen. He is well, sir?
Proph. The gods preserve him ever: yet,
deare beauty,
I finde some alteration in him lately,
     Since his returne to Sparta. — My
good lord,
I pray use no delay.
Bass. We had not needed
     An invitation, if his sisters health
Had not fallen into question. — Hast,
Penthea,
Slacke notaminute: lead the way, good
Prophilus;
I'le follow step by step.
Proph. Your arme, faire madam.
Exeunt omnes sed Bass. & Grau. Bass.
One word with your old bawdship: th'
hadst bin better Raild at the sinnes thou
worshipst then have thwarted My will:
Fle use thee cursedly. *Grau.* You dote,
You are beside yourselfe. A politician
150
     In jealousie? No, y'are too grosse, too
vulgar.
Pish, teach not me my trade; I know my
cue:
My crossing you sinks me into her trust,
By which I shall know all: my trade's a
sure one.
Bass. Forgive me, Grausis, twas consid-
eration 155 I rellisht not; but have a care
now.
Grau. Feare not,
I am no new-come-too't.
_ *Bass.* Thy life's upon it,
     And so is mine. My agonies are infi-
nite.
Exeunt omnes. SCAENE 2. *The palace.
Modes' apartment. Enter Ithocles
alone.*
Ithocles. Ambition! 'tis of vipers breed;
it
knawes
A passage through the wombe that gave
it motion.

148 *linnet.* G-D, saints. 155 *Grausis. Q,*
GranIu.

Ambition, like *a.* seeled dove, mounts
upward,
Higher and higher still to pearch on
clouds,
But tumbles headlong downe with
heavier mine.
So squibs and crackers flye into the
ayre,
Then, onely breaking with a noyse, they
vanish
In stench and smoke. Morality appli'd
To timely practice keeps the soule in
tune,
At whose sweet musicke all our actions
dance:
But this is forme of books and schoole-
tradi-
tion;
    It physicks not the sicknesse of a
minde
Broken with griefes: strong feavers are
not eas'd
With counsell, but with best receipts
and
meanes: Meanes, speedy meanes and
certaine; that's the cure.
*Enter Armostes and Crotolon. Ar-
mostes.* You sticke, Lord Crotolon, upon a point
Too   nice   and   too   unnecessary.
Prophilus
Is every way desertfull. I am confident
Your wisdome is too ripe to need in-
struction
From your sonnes tutillage.
Crotolon. Yet not so ripe,
    My Lord Armostes, that it dares to
dote Upon the painted meat of smooth
perswasion, Which tempts me to a
breach of faith.
Itho. Not yet
Resolv'd, my lord? Why, if your sonnes
consent
Be so availeable, wee'll write to Athens
25
    For his repaire to Sparta. The kings
hand
Will joyne with our desires; he has
beene mov'd too't.
Armo. Yes, and the king himselfe im-
portun'd
    Crotolon For a dispatch.
Crot. Kings may command; their wils

Are lawes not to be questioned.
Itho. By this marriage 30
You knit an union so devout, so hearty,
Betweene your loves to me and mine to
yours,
As if mine owne blood had an interest
in it;
For Prophilus is mine, and I am his.
Crot. My lord, my lord! — *Ith.* What,
good sir? speak your thought. 35 *Crot.*
Had this sincerity beene reall once, My
Orgilus had not beene now un-wiv'd,
Nor your lost sister buried in a bride-
bed: Your unckle here, Armostes,
knowes this truth; For had your father
Thrasus liv'd, — but peace 40 Dwell in
his grave! I have done.
Armo. Y'are bold and bitter. *Itbo.* 'A
presses home the injury; it smarts: No
reprehensions, uncle, I deserve 'em.
Yet, gentle sir, consider what the heat
Of an unsteady youth, a giddy braine,
45 Greene indiscretion, flattery of greatnesse,
Rawnesse of judgement, wilfulnesse in
folly,
    Thoughts vagrant as the wind, and as
uncertaine,
    Might lead a boy in yeeres too: 'twas
a fault,
    A capitall fault; for then I could not
dive 5
    Into the secrets of commanding love:
    Since when, experience, by the ex-
tremities in others, Hath forc'd me to
collect, and, trust me, Crot- olon,
    I will redeeme those wrongs with any
service Your satisfaction can require for
currant. 55 *Armo,* Thy acknowledgement is satisfaction. What would you
more?
Crot. I'me conquer'd: if Euphrania
Her selfe admit the motion, let it be so.
I doubt not my sonnes liking.
Itho. Use my fortunes,
    Life, power, sword, and heart, all are
your   owne.   60   *Enter   Bassanes,
Prophilus,   Calantha,   Penthea,   Euphranea,   Chrystalla,   Philema,   and
Grausis. Armo.* The princesse with your
sister.
Calantha. I present 'ee
A stranger here in court, my lord; for
did not
Desire of seeing you draw her abroad,

We had not beene made happy in her
company.
52 *the extremities.* G-D, th extremes.
56 *Thy acknowledgement.* G-D, Th" acknowledgment. *Itho.* You are a gracious
princesse. — Sister, wedlocke 65
Holds too severe a passion in your na-
ture,
Which can engrosse all duty to your
husband,
Without attendance on so deare a mis-
tresse.
'Tis not my brothers pleasure, I pre-
sume,
T' immure her in a chamber.
Bassanes. 'Tis her will; 7
    Shee   governes   her   owne   houres.
Noble Ithocles,
We thanke the gods for your successe
and welfare.
Our lady has of late beene indispos'd,
Else we had waited on you with the
first.
Itho. How does Penthea now?
Penthea. You best know, brother, 75
From whom my health and comforts are
deriv'd.
Bass. aside. I like the answer well: 'tis
sad and modest.
There may be tricks yet, tricks. — Have
an eye, Grausis!
Cal. Now, Crotolon, the suit we joyn'd
in must not Fall by too long demurre.
Crot. 'Tis granted, princesse, 80
For my part.
Armo. With condition, that his sonne
Favour the contract.
Cal. Such delay is easie.
The joyes of marriage make thee,
Prophilus,
    A proud deserver of Euphrania's
love,
And her of thy desert..
Proph. Most sweetly gracious! 5 *Bass.*
The joyes of marriage are the heaven on
earth,
    Life's paradise, great princesse, the
soules quiet,
Sinewes of concord, earthly immortali-
ty,
Eternity of pleasures; no restoratives
Like to a constant woman!—*Aside.* But
where
is she? 90
    'Twould puzzle all the gods but to

create

Such a new monster. — I can speake by proofe,

For I rest in Elizium; 'tis my happinesse.

Crot. Euphrania, how are you resolv'd, speake

freely,

In your affections to this gentleman?

95 *Euphranea.* Nor more nor lesse then as his love assures me,

Which, if your liking with my brothers warrants,

I cannot but approve in all points worthy.

Crot. So, so, I know your answer.

Itho. 'T had bin pitty

To sunder hearts so equally consented. 100 *Enter Hemopbill. Hemophil.* The king, Lord Ithocles, commands your presence; And, fairest princesse, yours.

CaL We will attend him. *Enter Groneas. Groneas.* Where are the lords? All must unto the king Without delay: the Prince of Argos — *CaL* Well, sir. *Gron.* Is comming to the court, sweet lady.

Cal. How! 105

The Prince of Argos?

Gron. 'Twas my fortune, madam, T'enjoy the honour of these happy tidings.

Itho. Penthea!

Pen. Brother!

Itho. Let me an howre hence

Meet you alone within the palace grove;

I have some secret with you.—Prethe, friend, no

Conduct her thither, and have speciall care

The walks be clear'd of any to disturbe us.

Propb. I shall.

Bass. How's that?

Itho. Alone, pray be alone. —

I am your creature, princesse. — On, my lords!

Exeunt except Banana.

Bassanes.

Bass. Alone! alone! what meanes that word

"alone"? 115

Why might not I be there? — hum!

— hee's her brother; Brothers and sisters are but flesh and blood,

And this same whorson court ease is temptation

To a rebellion in the veines. — Besides, His fine friend Prophilus must be her guardian. i»o

Why may not he dispatch a businesse nimbly

Before the other come? — or—pandring, pan-

dring

For one another, bee't to sister, mother,

Wife, couzen, any thing, 'mongst youths of

mettall

Is in request. It is so — stubborne fate: 125

But if I be a cuckold, and can know it,

I will be fell, and fell.

Re-center Groneas. Gron. My lord, y'are call'd for.

Bass. Most hartily I thanke ye. Where's my wife, pray? *Gron.* Retir'd amongst the ladies—

Bass. Still I thanke 'ee:

There's an old waiter with her; saw you her too? 130

Gron. She sits i'th presence lobby fast asleepe,

sir.

Bass. Asleepe? sleepe, sir!

Gron. Is your lordship troubled?

You will not to the king?

Bass. Your humblest vassaile. *Gron.* Your servant, my good lord.

Bass. I wait your footsteps.

Exeunt. SCAENE THE THIRD. *The gardens of the palace. Propbilus, Penthea. Propbilus.* In this walke, lady, will your brother find you:

And, with your favour, give me leave a little

To worke a preparation. In his fashion I have observ'd of late some kind of slacknesse

To such alacrity as nature 5

And custome tooke delight in: sadnesse growes

Upon his recreations, which he hoards In such a willing silence, that to question

The grounds will argue little skill in

friendship,

And lesse good manners.

Penthea. Sir, I'me not inquisitive 10

Of secrecies without an invitation.

Proph. With pardon, lady, not a sillable Of mine implyes so rude a sense; the drift —

Enter Orgilus, disguised as before,

Proph. Doe thy best

To make this lady merry for an houre.

Exit. 15

Orgilus. Your will shall be a law, sir.

Pen. Prethe, leave me;

I have some private thoughts I would account with: Use thou thine owne.

5 G-D supplies once after *nature.* 9 *little.* Supplied by G-D. *Org.* Speake on, faire nimph, our soules Can dance as well to musicke of the spheares As any's who have feasted with the gods. 20 *Pen.* Your schoole terms are too troublesome. *Org.* What heaven Refines mortality from drosse of earth But such as uncompounded beauty hallowes

With glorified perfection.

Pen. Set thy wits

In a lesse wild proportion.

Org. Time can never 5

On the white table of unguilty faith Write counterfeit dishonour; turne those eyes,

The arrowes of pure love, upon that fire Which once rose to a flame, perfum'd with

vowes

As sweetly scented as the incense smoking 30

On Vesta's altars,.........

. the holiest odours, virgin teares, sprinkled, like dewes, to feed 'em, And to increase their fervour. *Pen.* Be not franticke. *Org.* All pleasures are but meere imagination, 35 Feeding the hungry appetite with steame, 31-33 *On Pesta't... to feed 'em.* So arranged by G. In Q this passage appears thus:

The holiest Artars, Virgin teares (like On *ytstas* odours) sprinkled dewa to feed 'em,

And sight of banquet, whilst the body pines,

Not relishing the reall tast of food: Such is the leannesse of a heart divided

From entercourse of troth-contracted loves; 4.0

No horror should deface that precious figure

Seal'd with the lively stampe of equall soules.

Pen. Away! some fury hath bewitch'd thy tongue:

The breath of ignorance that flyes from thence,

Ripens a knowledge in me of afflictions 45

Above all suffrance. — Thing of talke, be gone!

Be gone, without reply!

Org. Be just, Penthea,

In thy commands: when thou send'st forth a doome

Of banishment, know first on whom it lights. Thus I take off the shrowd, in which my cares 5 Are folded up from view of common eyes.

Tbrows of bis scholar's dress. What is thy sentence next? *Pen.* Rash man, thou layest

A blemish on mine honour, with the hazard

Of thy too desperate life: yet I professe,

By all the lawes of ceremonious wed-locke, 55

I have not given admittance to one thought

Of female change since cruelty enforc'd

Divorce betwixt my body and my heart:

Why would you fall from goodnesse thus?

Org. O, rather

Examine me how I could live to say 60

I have bin much, much wrong'd. 'Tis for thy sake

I put on this imposture: deare Penthea,

If thy soft bosome be not turn'd to marble,

Thou't pitty our calamities; my interest

Confirmes me thou art mine still.

Pen. Lend your hand; 65

With both of mine I claspe it thus; thus kisse it; Thus kneele before ye.

Org. You instruct my duty. *Pen.* We may stand up. Have you ought else to urge

Of new demand? As for the old, forget it;

'Tis buried in an everlasting silence, 7

And shall be, shall be ever; what more would ye?

Org. I would possesse my wife; the equity Of very reason bids me.

Pen. Is that all? *Org.* Why 'tis the all of me my selfe. *Pen.* Remove

Your steps some distance from me; at this space 75

A few words I dare change; but first put on

Your borrowed shape.

Org. You are obey'd; 'tis done.

Pen. How, Orgilus, by promise I was thine The heavens doe witnesse; they can witnesse too

A rape done on my truth: how I doe love thee go

Yet, Orgilus, and yet, must best appeare

In tendering thy freedome; for I find

The constant preservation of thy merit,

By thy not daring to attempt my fame

With injury of any loose conceit, 85

Which might give deeper wounds to discontents.

Continue this faire race; then, though I cannot

Adde to thy comfort, yet I shall more often

Remember from what fortune I am fallen,

And pitty mine owne ruine. — Live, live happy, 90

Happy in thy next choyce, that thou maist

people

This barren age with vertues in thy issue!

And O, when thou art married, thinke on me

"With mercy, not contempt! I hope thy wife,

Hearing my story, will not scorne my fall. 95

Now let us part.

Org. Part! yet advise thee better:

Penthea is the wife to Orgilus,

And ever shall be.

Pen, Never shall nor will.

Org. How! *Pen.* Heare me; in a word

I'le tell thee why: The virgin dowry which my birth bestow'd 100

Is ravish'd by another: my true love

Abhorres to thinke that Orgilus deserv'd

No better favours then a second bed.

Org. I must not take this reason.

Pen. To confirme it;

Should I outlive my bondage, let me meet 105

Another worse then this and lesse desir'd,

If of all the men alive thou shouldst but touch

My lip or hand againe!

Org. Penthea, now

I tell 'ee, you grow wanton in my sufferance:

Come, sweet, th'art mine.

Pen. Uncivill sir, forbeare,no

Or I can turne affection into vengeance;

Your reputation, if you value any,

Lyes bleeding at my feet. Unworthy man,

If ever henceforth thou appeare in language,

Message, or letter to betray my frailty, n5

I'le call thy former protestations lust,

And curse my starres for forfeit of my judgement.

Goe thou, fit onely for disguise and walkes,

To hide thy shame: this once I spare thy life.

I laugh at mine owne confidence; my sorrowesi»o

By thee are made inferiour to my fortunes.

If ever thou didst harbour worthy love,

Dare not to answer. My good Genius guide me,

107 *the.* G-D omits.

That I may never see thee more! —

Goe from me. *Org.* I ' l e teare my vaile of politicke French off,,

And stand up like a man resolv'd to doe: Action, not words, shall shew me.

O Penthea! *Exit Orgtlus. Pen.* 'A sigh'd my name, sure, as he parted from me:

I feare I was too rough. Alas, poore gentleman,

'A look'd not like the ruines of his youth, 130

But like the ruines of those ruines. Honour,

How much we fight with weaknesse to preserve thee!

Enter Bassanes and Grausis,

Bassanes. Fye on thee! damb thee, rotten

magat, damb thee!

Sleepe? sleepe at court? and now? Aches, convulsions,

Impostumes, rhemes, gouts, palsies, clog thy

bones,j

A dozen yeeres more yet!

Grausis. Now y'are in humors. *Bass.* Shee's by her selfe, there's hope of that; shee's sad too;

Shee's in strong contemplation; yes, and fixt:

The signes are wholesome.

Grau. Very wholsome, truly.

Bass. Hold your chops, night mare! — Lady, come; your brother 140

Is carried to his closet; you must thither.

Pen. Not well, my lord? *Bass.* A sudden fit; 'twill off;

Some surfeit or disorder. — How doest, deerest?

Pen. Your newes is none o" th' best.

Re-enter Propbilus.

Propb. The chiefe of men,

The excellentest Ithocles, desires 145

Your presence, madam.

Bass. We are hasting to him. *Pen.* In vaine we labour in this course of life To piece our journey out at length, or crave Respite of breath; our home is in the grave. *Bass.* Perfect philosophy: then let us care 15$ To live so that our reckonings may fall even When w'are to make account. *Proph.* He cannot feare

Who builds on noble grounds: sicknesse or paine

Is the deservers exercise; and such

Your vertuous brother to the world is knowne. 155

Speake comfort to him, lady; be all gentle:

Starres fall but in the grossenesse of our sight;

A good man dying, th' earth doth lose a light.

Exeunt omnes. 150-152 *then let... account.* G-D gives this to Penthea.

ACTUS TERTIUS: SCAENA PRIMA. *The study of Tecnicus.*

Enter Tecnicus, and Orgilus in his owae shape.

Tecnicus. Be well advis'd; let not a resolution

Of giddy rashnesse choake the breath of reason.

Orgilus. It shall not, most sage master.

Teen. I am jealous:

For if the borrowed shape so late put on

Inferr'd a consequence, we must conclude 5

Some violent designe of sudden nature

Hath shooke that shadow off, to flye upon

A new-hatch'd execution. Orgilus,

Take heed thou hast not, under our integrity,

Shrowded unlawfull plots: our mortall eyes 10

Pierce not the secrets of your hearts; the gods

Are onely privie to them.

Org. Learned Tecnicus,

Such doubts are causelesse; and to cleere the truth From misconceit, the present state commands me.

The Prince of Argos comes himselfe in person 15 In quest of great Calantha for his bride, II *hearu.* G-D, heart.

Our kingdomes heire; besides, mine onely sister

Euphrania is dispos'd to Prophilus;

Lastly, the king is sending letters for me

To Athens for my quicke repaire to court: 2o

Please to accept these reasons.

Teen. Just ones, Orgilus.

Not to be contradicted: yet beware Of an unsure foundation; no faire colours

Can fortifie a building faintly joynted.

I have observ'd a growth in thy aspect »5

Of dangerous extent, sudden, and, looke too't!

I might adde certaine —

Org. My aspect? Could art

Runne through mine inmost thoughts, it should not sift

An inclination there more then what suited

With justice of mine honour.

Teen. I beleeve it. 30

But know then, Orgilus, what honour is:

Honour consists not in a bare opinion

By doing any act that feeds content;

Brave in appearance, 'cause we thinke it brave:

Such honour comes by accident, not nature, 35

Proceeding from the vices of our passion,

Which makes our reason drunke. But reall

honour

Is the reward of vertue, and acquir'd By justice or by valour which for bases

Hath justice to uphold it. He then failes 40

In honour, who for lucre or revenge Commits thefts, murthers, treasons, and adulteries,

With such like, by intrenching on just lawes,

Whose sov'raignty is best preserv'd by justice.

Thus, as you see how honour must be grounded 45

On knowledge, not opinion,— for opinion

Relyes on probability and accident,

But knowledge on necessity and truth,

—

I leave thee to the fit consideration Of what becomes the grace of reall honour, 50

Wishing successe to all thy vertuous meanings.

Org. The gods increase thy wisdome, reverend oracle, And in thy precepts make me ever thrifty!

Exit Org. Tecn. I thanke thy wish. — Much mystery of fate

Lyes hid in that mans fortunes; curiosity 55

May lead his actions into rare attempts;

But let the gods be moderators still;

No humane power can prevent their will.

Enter Armostes.

From whence come 'ee?

Armostes. From King Amyclas, — pardon My interruption of your studies. — Here, 6 41 *or.* So G-D. Q, of.

In this seal'd box, he sends a treasure dcare

To him as his crowne; 'a prayes your gravity

You would examine, ponder, sift, and

bolt
The pith and circumstance of every tittle
The scroll within containes.

Teen. What is't, Armostes? 65 *Armo.* It
is the health of Sparta, the kings life,
Sinewes and safety of the common-
wealth; The summe of what the oracle
deliver'd When last he visited the
propheticke temple At Delphos: what
his reasons are for which 70 After so
long a silence he requires You counsaile
now, grave man, his majesty Will soone
himselfe acquaint you with.

Teen. Apollo
Inspire my intellect! —The Prince of
Argos
Is entertain'd?

Armo. He is; and has demanded 75
Our princesse for his wife; which I
conceive
One speciall cause the king importunes
you
For resolution of the oracle.

Teen. My duty to the king, good peace
to
   Sparta,
And faire day to Armostes!

Armo. Like to Tecnicus! So *Exeunt.*
SCENA SECUNDA. *Modes'apartment in
the paiace. Soft musicke. A song.*

Can you paint a thought? or number
Every fancy in a slumber?
Can you count soft minutes roving
From a dyals point by moving?
Can you graspe a sigh? or, lastly,
Rob a virgins honour chastly?
No, O, no! yet you may
Sooner doe both that and this,
This and that, and never misse,
Then by any praise display
Beauties beauty, such a glory
As beyond all fate, all story,
All armes, all arts,
All loves, all hearts,
Greater then those, or they, 1 Doe,
shall, and must obey. Duringwhich time,
*euters*Prophilus, *Bassanes, Penthea,*
Grausis,passing over the stage,-Bas-
sanes and Grau-sis enter againe softly,
stealing to several! stands, and listen.

Bassanes. All silent, calme, secure.—
Grausis, no creaking f No noyse? dost
heare nothing?

Grausis. Not a mouse,
Or whisper of the winde.

Bass. The floore is matted,
The bed-posts sure are steele or marble.
— Soul- diers
   Should not affect, me thinkes,
straines so effeminate;
   Sounds of such delicacy are but
fawnings
Upon the sloth of luxury: they heighten
Cinders of covert lust up to a flame.

Grau. What doe you meane, my lord?
Speak low; that gabling »5
   Of yours will but undoe us.

Bass. Chamber-combats
Are felt, not hard.

Pro. within. 'A wakes.

Bass. What's that?

Ithodes within. Who's there
Sister? All quit the roome else.

Bass. 'Tis consented! *Re-enter Propbilus.*

Proph. Lord Bassanes, your brother
would be
private,
We must forbeare; his sleepe hath newly left
him. _ 30
Please 'ee withdraw?

Bass. By any meanes; 'tis fit. *Proph.*
Pray, gentlewoman, walke too.

Grau. Yes, I will, sir.

*Exeunt omnes. The scene opens; Itho-
cles discovered in a cbayre, and Pentbea. Itho.* Sit nearer, sister, to me; nearer yet. We had one father, in one wombe
tooke life, Were brought up twins together, yet have liv'd 35 At distance
like two strangers. I could wish That the
first pillow whereon I was cradell'd Had
prov'd to me a grave. *Pentbea.* You had
beene happy:
Then had you never knowne that sinne
of life
Which blots all following glories with a
vengeance, 40
For forfeiting the last will of the dead,
From whom you had your being.

Itho. Sad Penthea,
   Thou canst not be too cruell; my rash
spleene
H ath with a violent hand pluck'd from
thy bosome
A lover-blest heart, to grind it into dust,
45
   For which mine's now a breaking.

Pen. Not yet, heaven,

I doe beseech thee! first let some wild
fires
Scorch, not consume it; may the heat be
cherisht
With desires infinite, but hopes impossible!

Itho. Wrong'd soule, thy prayers are
heard.

Pen. Here, lo, I breathe 50
A miserable creature, led to ruine
By an unnaturall brother.

45 lover-blest. G-D, love-blest.

Itho. I consume
In languishing affections for that tres-
passe,
Yet cannot dye.

Pen. The handmaid to the wages
   Of country toyle drinkes the untrou-
bled streames 55
With leaping kids and with the bleating
lambes,
And so allayes her thirst secure, whiles
I
Quench my hot sighes with fleetings of
my teares.

Itho. The labourer doth eat his coursest
bread, Earn'd with his sweat, and lyes
him downe to sleepe; o
   Which every bit I touch turnes in di-
gestion
To gall as bitter as Penthea's curse.
Put me to any pennance for my tyranny,
And I will call thee mercifull.

Pen. Pray kill me,
   Rid me from living with a jealous
husband; 65 Then we will joyne in
friendship, be againe Brother and sister.
— Kill me, pray; nay, will'ee?

Itho. How does thy lord esteeme thee?

Pen. Such an one
As onely you have made me; a faith-
breaker,
A spotted whore: forgive me, I am one
70
   In act, not in desires, the gods must
witnesse.

55 Of... streames. So arranged by G. *Q,*
the untroubled of country toyle, drinkes
streames. 61 *Which.* G-D While, *diges-
tion.* Q, disgestion. 71 *act.* Q, art. *Itho.*
Thou dost be lye thy friend. *Pen.* I doe
not, Ithocles;
For she that's wife to Orgilus, and lives
In knowne adultery with Bassanes,
Is at the best a whore. Wilt kill me now?

75

The ashes of our parents will assume
Some dreadfull figure, and appeare to
charge
Thy bloody gilt, that hast betray'd their
name
To infamy in this reproachfull match.
Itho. After my victories abroad, at home
80
I meet despaire; ingratitude of nature
Hath made my actions monstrous: thou
shalt
stand
A deity, my sister, and be worship'd
For thy resolved martyrdome; wrong'd
maids
And married wives shall to thy hal-
lowed shrine 85
Offer their orisons, and sacrifice
Pure turtles crown'd with mirtle, if thy
pitty
Unto a yeelding brothers pressure lend
One finger but to ease it.
Pen. O, no more!
Itho. Death waits to waft me to the Sty-
gian bankes, 90
And free me from this chaos of my
bondage;
And till thou wilt forgive, I must indure.
Pen. Who is the saint you serve?
Itho. Friendship, or nearnesse 93 *near-*
nas. Supplied from G-D.
Of birth to any but my sister, durst not
Have mov'd that question as a secret,
sister: 95
I dare not murmure to my selfe.
Pen. Let me,
By your new protestations I conjure 'ee,
Partake her name.
Itho. Her name, — 'tis, — 'tis, I dare
not.
Pen. All your respects are forg'd. *Itho.*
They are not. — Peace!
Calantha is the princesse, the kings
daughter, too
Sole heire of Sparta. — Me most miser-
able!
Doe I now love thee? for my injuries
Revenge thy selfe with bravery, and
gossip
My treasons to the kings eares. Doe;
Calantha
Knowes it not yet, nor Prophilus, my
nearest. 105
Pen. Suppose you were contracted to

her, would it not
Split even your very soule to see her
father
Snatch her out of your armes against her
will,
And force her on the Prince of Argos?
Itho. Trouble not
The fountaines of mine eyes with
thine owne story; no
I sweat in blood for't.
Pen. We are reconcil'd:
Alas, sir, being children, but two
branches 95 *question ... shter.* G-D puts
a semicolon after *yugstion*, changes *at*
to *'tis,* and puts a comma after *aster.*
Of one stocke, 'tis not fit we should
divide:
Have comfort, you may find it.
It ho. Yes, in thee:
Onely in thee, Penthea mine.
Pen. If sorrowes n$
Have not too much dull'd my infected
braine,
I'le cheere invention for an active
straine.
Itho. Mad man! why have I wrong'd a
maid so excellent!
Enter Bassanes with a ponyard,
Prophilus, Groneas,
Hemopbill, and Grausis.
Bass. I can forbeare no longer; more, I
will not:
Keepe off your hands, or fall upon my
point, no
Patience is tye'd, for like a slow-pac'd
asse
Ye ride my easie nature, and proclaime
My sloth to vengeance a reproach and
property.
Itho. The meaning of this rudenesse?
Proph. Hee's distracted. *Pen.* O my
griev'd lord! *Grau.* Sweet lady, come
not neere him 5115
He holds his perilous weapon in his
hand
To pricke "a cares not whom, nor
where, — see,
see, see!
Bass. My birth is noble: though the popular blast
Of vanity, as giddy as thy youth,
Hath rear'd thy name up to bestride a
cloud, 130
Or progresse in the chariot of the
sunne,

I am no clod of trade, to lackey pride,
Nor, like your slave of expectation,
wait
The baudy hinges of your dores, or
whistle
For mysticall conveyance to your
bed-sports. 135 *Groneas.* Fine humors!
They become him.
Hemophil. How 'a stares,
Struts, puffes, and sweats: most ad-
mirable lunacy!
Itho. But that I may conceive the spirit
of wine
Has tooke possession of your soberer
custome,
I'de say you were unmannerly.
Pen. Deare brother! 140 *Bass.* Unman-
nerly!—Mew, kitling!—Smooth for-
mality
Is usher to the ranknesse of the blood,
But impudence beares up the traine. In-
deed,
sir,
Your fiery mettall or your springall
blaze
Of huge renowne is no sufficient royalty
14J
To print upon my forehead the
scorne, " cuckold."
Itho. His jealousie has rob'd him of his
wits; 'A talkes 'a knowes not what.
Bass. Yes, and 'a knowes
To whom 'a talkes; to one that franks
his lust
In swine-security of bestiall incest.
Itho. Hah, devill!
5(?w. I will hallo't, though I blush more
To name the filthinesse than thou to act
it. *Itho.* Monster! *Draws his sword.*
Proph. Sir, by our friendship — *Pen.* By
our bloods,
Will you quite both undoe us, brother?
Grau, Out on him,
These are his megrims, firks, and
melancholies. 155 *Hem.* Well said, old
touch-hole.
Gron. Kick him out at dores. *Pen.* With
favour, let me speake. — My lord, what
slacknesse
In my obedience hath deserv'd this
rage?
Except humility and silent duty
Have drawne on your unquiet, my sim-
plicity 160
Ne're studied your vexation.

Bass. Light of beauty,

Deale not ungently with a desperate wound!

No breach of reason dares make warre with her

Whose lookes are soveraignty, whose breath is

balme:

O that I could preserve thee in fruition 165

As in devotion!

Pen. Sir, may every evill

Lock'd in Pandora's box, showre, in your presence, On my unhappy head, if since you made me 159 *silent.* So G-D. Q, siulcnt.

A partner in your bed, I have beene faulty

In one unseemely thought against your honour. 170

Itho. Purge not his griefes, Penthea.

Bass. Yes, say on,

Excellent creature! — Good, be not a hinderance

To peace and praise of vertue. — O my senses

Are charm'd with sounds caelestiall! — On,

deare, on;

I never gave you one ill word; say, did I? 175 Indeed I did not.

Pen. Nor, by Juno's forehead,

Was I e're guilty of a wanton error.

Bass. O goddesse! let me kneele.

Grau. Alas, kind animall.

Itho. No, but for pennance.

Bass. Noble sir, what is it?

With gladnesse I embrace it; yet, pray let not 180

My rashnesse teach you to be too unmercifull!.

Itho. When you shall shew good proofe that

manly wisdome,

Not over-sway'd by passion or opinion,

Knowes how to lead your judgement, then

this lady,

Your wife, my sister, shall returne in safety g

Home to be guided by you; but, till first

I can out of cleare evidence approve it,

Shee shall be my care.

184 *your.* Supplied from G-D.

Bass. Rip my bosome up,

Ple stand the execution with a constancy:

This torture is unsufferable.

Itho. Well, sir, 190

I dare not trust her to your fury.

Bass. But

Penthea sayes not so.

Pen. She needs no tongue

To plead excuse who never purpos'd wrong.

Hem. Virgin of reverence and antiquity, Stay you behind. 195

Gron. The court wants not your diligence.

Exeunt omnes, ted Bass. £3" *Graus.*

Grau. What will you doe, my lord? my lady's gone;

I am deny'd to follow.

Bass. I may see her,

Or speake to her once more.

Grau. And feele her too, man;

Be of good chcare, she's your owne flesh and bone. 200 *Bass.* Diseases desperate must find cures alike: She swore she has beene true.

Grau. True, on my modesty. *Bass.* Let him want truth who credits not her vowes!

Much wrong I did her, but her brother infinite; Rumor will voyce me the contempt of manhood, 205

Should I run on thus. Some way I must try

To out-doe art, and jealousie decry.

Exeunt omnes. SCENA TERTIA. *A room in the palace. Flourish. Enter Amyclas, Nearchus leading Calantha, Armostes, Crotolon, Euphranea, Cbristalla, Pbilema, and Amelus. Amyclas.* Cozen of Argos, what the heavens have pleas'd

In their unchanging counsels to conclude

For both ourkingdomesweale,wemust submit to:

Nor can we be unthankful! to their bounties,

Who, when we were even creeping to our

graves,

Sent us a daughter, in whose birth our hope

Continues of succession. As you are

In title next, being grandchilde to our aunt,

So we in heart desire you may sit nearest

Calantha's love; since we have ever vow'd i

Not to inforce affection by our will,

But by her owne choyce to confirme it gladly.

Nearchus. You speake the nature of a right just father. I come not hither roughly to demand 207 *jealousie decry.* Emendation made by G-D. Q cry a jealousie.

5 *graves.* So Q and G; changed by D in G-D *to grave.*

My cozens thraldome, but to free mine owne: 15

Report of great Calantha's beauty, vertue,

Sweetnesse, and singular perfections, courted

All eares to credit what I finde was publish'd

By constant truth: from which, if any service

Of my desert can purchase faire construction, »o

This lady must command it.

Calantha. Princely sir,

So well you know how to professe observance

That you instruct your hearers to become

Practitioners in duty; of which number I'le study to be chiefe.

Near. Chiefe, glorious virgine, 5

In my devotions, as in all mens wonder.

Amy. Excellent cozen, we deny no libertie;

Use thine owne opportunities.—Armostes,

We must consult with the philosophers; The businesse is of weight.

Armostes. Sir, at your pleasure. 3 *Amy.* You told me, Crotolon, your sonne's return'd

From Athens: wherefore comes 'a not to court

As we commanded?

Crotolon. He shall soone attend

Your royall will, great sir.

Amy. The marriage

Betweene young Prophilus and Euphranea, 35

Tasts of too much delay.

Crot. My lord — *Amy.* Some pleasures
At celebration of it would give life
To th' entertainment of the prince our kinsman;
Our court weares gravity more then we rellish.
Arm, Yet the heavens smile on all your high attempts, 40
Without a cloud.
Crot. So may the gods protect us! *Cal.*
A prince, a subject? *Near.* Yes, to beauties scepter;
As all hearts kneele, so mine.
Cal. You are too courtly. *Enter to them, Itbocles, Orgilus, Propbilus. Ithocles.*
Your safe returne to Sparta is most welcome;
I joy to meet you here, and as occasion 45
Shall grant us privacy, will yeeld you reasons
Why I should covet to deserve the title
Of your respected friend; for without complement
Beleeve it, Orgilus, 'tis my ambition.
Orgilus. Your lordship may command me, your poore servant. 50 *Itho. aside.*
So amorously close? — So soone? — my heart!
Prophilus. What sudden change is next? 51 *close. Q,* close close. *Itho.* Life to the king,
To whom I here present this noble gentleman, New come from Athens; royall sir, vouchsafe Your gracious hand in favour of his merit. 55 *Crot. aside.* My sonne preferr'd by Ithocles!
Amy. Our bounties
Shall open to thee, Orgilus; for instance, —

Harke in thine eare,— if out of those inventions
Which flow in Athens, thou hast there ingrost
Some rarity of wit to grace the nuptials 60
Of thy faire sister, and renowne our court
In th' eyes of this young prince, we shall be
debtor
To thy conceit; thinke on't.
Org. Your highnesse honors me.
Near. My tongue and heart are twins.
Cal. A noble birth,

Becomming such a father. — Worthy Orgilus, 65 You are a guest most wish'd for.
Org. May my duty
Still rise in your opinion, sacred princesse!
Itho. Euphranea's brother, sir, a gentleman Well worthy of your knowledge.
Near. We embrace him,
Proud of so deare acquaintance.
Amy. All prepare 7
For revels and disport; the joyes of Hymen,
Like Phoebus in his lustre, puts to flight
All mists of dulnesse; crowne the houres with gladnesse;
No sounds but musicke, no discourse but mirth. *Cal.* Thine arme, I prethe, Ithocles. —
Nay, good
My lord, keepe on your way; I am provided.
Near. I dare not disobey.
Itho. Most heavenly lady! *Exeunt.*
SCENA QUARTA. *A room in the house of Crotolon.*
Enter Crotolon, Orgilus. Crotolon. The king hath spoke his mind.
Orgilus. His will he hath;
But were it lawfull to hold plea against
The power of greatnesse, not the reason, haply
Such under-shrubs as subjects sometimes might
Borrow of nature justice, to informe 5
That licence soveraignty holds without checke
Over a meeke obedience.
Crot. How resolve you
Touching your sisters marriage? Prophilus
Is a deserving and a hopefull youth.
Org. I envy not his merit, but applaud it; 10 Could wish him thrift in all his best desires, And with a willingnesse inleague our blood II *viisX.* So G-D. *Q,* with.
With his, for purchase of full growth in friendship.
He never touch'd on any wrong that malic'd
The honour of our house, nor stirr'd our peace; 15
Yet, with your favour, let me not forget
Under whose wing he gathers warmth

and comfort,
Whose creature he is bound, made, and must
live so.
Crot. Sonne, sonne, I find in thee a harsh
condition;
No curtesie can winne it; 'tis too ranckorous. o *Org.* Good sir, be not severe in your construction;
I am no stranger to such easie calmes
As sit in tender bosomes: lordly Ithocles
Hath grac'd my entertainment in abundance;
Too humbly hath descended from that height 25
Of arrogance and spleene which wrought the
rape
On griev'd Penthea's purity: his scorne
Of my untoward fortunes is reclaim'd
Unto a courtship, almost to a fawning:
I'le kisse his foot, since you will have it so. 30
Crot. Since I will have it so? Friend, I will
have it so
Without our ruine by your politike plots,
Or wolfe of hatred snarling in your breast.
You have a spirit, sir, have ye? a familiar
That poasts i'th' ayre for your intelligence? 35
Some such hobgoblin hurried you from Athens,
For yet you come unsent for. 29 *courtihip. Q,* coutship.
Org. If unwelcome,
I might have found a grave there.
Crot. Sure, your businesse
Was soone dispatch'd, or your mind alter'd quickly.
Org. 'Twas care, sir, of my health cut short my journey; 4
For there a generall infection
Threatens a desolation.
Crot. And I feare
Thou hast brought backe a worse infection with thee,
Infection of thy mind; which, as thou sayst, Threatens the desolation of our family. 45 *Org.* Forbid it, our deare Ge-

nius! I will rather

Be made a sacrifice on Thrasus monument,
Or kneele to Ithocles his sonne in dust,
Then wooe a fathers curse. My sisters marriage
With Prophilus is from my heart confirm'd: 5
May I live hated, may I dye despis'd,
If I omit to further it in all
That can concerne me!

Scene iv. E&e Broken Jeart 209 *Grot,*
I have beene too rough.

My duty to my king made me so earnest;
Excuse it Orgilus.

Org. Deare sir,— *Enter to them, Prophilus, Euphranea, Ithocles, Groneas, Hemophil. Crot.* Here comes 55

Euphranea, with Prophilus and Ithocles.

Org. Most honored! — ever famous!
Ithocles. Your true friend;
On earth not any truer. — With smooth eyes
Looke on this worthy couple; your consent
Can onely make them one.

Org. They have it. — Sister, 60

Thou pawn'dst to me an oath, of which ingage- ment
I never will release thee, if thou aym'st
At any other choyce then this.

Euphranea. Deare brother,
At him or none.

Crot. To which my blessing's added.
Org. Which, till a greater ceremony perfect, 65 Euphranea, lend thy hand; here, take her, Prophilus:
Live long a happy man and wife; and further, That these in presence may conclude an omen, Thus for a bridall song I close my wishes: *Comforts lasting, loves increasing, 70 Like soft houres never ceasing; Plenties pleasure, peace complying Witbout jarres, or tongues envying; Hearts by holy union wedded More then theirs by custome tedded; j Fruitful! issues; life so graced, Not by age to be defaced. Budding, as the yeare ensu'th, Every spring another youth: All what thought can adde beside 80 Croeone this bridegroome and this bride!*

Prophilus. You have seal'd joy close to my soule: Euphranea, Now I may call thee mine. *Itho.* I but exchange
One good friend for another.
Org. If these gallants
Will please to grace a poore invention g
By joyning with me in some slight devise,
I'le venture on a straine my younger dayes
Have studied for delight.
Hemopbil. With thankfull willingnesse
I offer my attendance; *Groneas.* No endevour
Of mine shall faile to shew itselfe.
Itbo. We will 90
All joyne to wait on thy directions, Orgilus.
Org. O, my good lord, your favours flow towards
A too unworthy worme; but as you please;
I am what you will shape me.
Itho. A fast friend.
Crot. I thanke thee, sonne, for this acknowledgement; 95 It is a sight of gladnesse. *Org,* But my duty. *Exeunt omnes.*
SCENA QUINTA *Calantha's apartment in the palace. Enter Calantha, Penthea, Cbristalla, Philema. Calantha.* Who e're would speake with us, deny his entrance; Be carefull of our charge.
Christalla. We shall, madam. *Cal.* Except the king himselfe, give none admittance; Not any. *Philema.* Madam, it shall be our care. *Exeunt Cbristalla and Philema. Calantha, Penthea. Cal.* Being alone, Penthea, you have granted 5
The oportunity you sought, and might
At all times have commanded. *Penthea.*
'Tis a benefit
Which I shall owe your goodnesse even in death for: My glasse of life, sweet princesse, hath few minutes
Remaining to runne downe; the sands are spent; 10
For by an inward messenger I feele
The summons of departure short and certaine.
Cat. You feed too much your melancholly.
Pen. Glories
Of humane greatnesse are but pleasing dreames
And shadowes soone decaying: on the

stage 15
Of my mortality my youth hath acted
Some scenes of vanity, drawne out at length
By varied pleasures, sweetned in the mixture,
But tragicall in issue: beauty, pompe,
With every sensuality our giddinesse
Doth frame an idoll, are unconstant friends
When any troubled passion makes assault
On the unguarded castle of the mind.
Cal. Contemne not your condition for thy proofe
Of bare opinion onely: to what end
Reach all these morall texts?
Pen. To place before ee
A perfect mirror, wherein you may see
How weary I am of a lingring life,
Who count the best a misery.
Cal. Indeed
You have no little cause: yet none so great 30 As to distrust a remedy.
Pen. That remedy
Must be a winding sheet, a fold of lead,
And some untrod-on corner in the earth.
Not to detaine your expectation, princesse,
I have an humble suit.
Cal. Speake; I enjoy it. *Pen.* Vouchsafe, then, to be my executrix, And take that trouble on 'ee to dispose Such legacies as I bequeath impartially: I have not much to give, the paines are easie; Heaven will reward your piety, and thanke it 40 When I am dead; for sure I must not live; I hope I cannot.
Cal. Now, beshrew thy sadnesse;
Xhou turn'st me too much woman.
Pen. aside . Her faire eyes
Melt into passion. — Then I have assurance Encouraging my boldnesse. — In this paper 45 My will was character'd; which you, with pardon, Shall now know from mine owne mouth.
Cal. Talke on, prethe;
It is a pretty earnest.
Pen. I have left me 35 *enjoy.* So *Q* and G-D. D suggests "enjoin." W. substitutes *and* for /.
But three poore jewels to bequeath. The first is
My youth; for though I am much old in griefes, 50 In yeares I am a child.

Cal. To whom that? *Pen.* To virgin-
wives, such as abuse not wed- locke
By freedome of desires, but covet
chiefly
The pledges of chast beds for tyes of
love,
Rather than ranging of their blood; and
next 55
To married maids, such as preferre the
number
Of honorable issue in their vertues
Before the flattery of delights by mar-
riage:
May those be ever young!
Cal. A second jewell
    You meane to part with.
Pen. 'Tis my fame, I trust 60
By scandall yet untouch'd; this I be-
queath
To Memory, and Times old daughter,
Truth.
If ever my unhappy name find mention
When I am falne to dust, may it deserve
Beseeming charity without dishonour.
g5
Cal. How handsomely thou playst with
harm- lesse sport
    Of meere imagination; speake the
last,
I strangely like thy will.
Pen. This jewell, madam, 51 To *whom*
that f G-D, To whom that jewel
    Scinev.j £lje ilBroben Jeart 215
    Is dearely precious to me; you must
use
The best of your discretion to imploy
This gift as I intend it.
Cal. Doe not doubt me.
Pen. 'Tis long agone since first I lost my
heart:
Long I have liv'd without it, else for
certaine
I should have given that too; but in stead
Of it, to great Calantha, Sparta's heire,
75
    By service bound and by affection
vow'd,
I doe bequeath in holiest rites of love
Mine onely brother, Ithocles.
Cal. What saydst thou?
Pen. Impute not, heaven-blest lady, to
ambition
A faith as humbly perfect as the prayers
80
    Of a devoted suppliant can indow it:

Looke on him, princesse, with an eye of
pitty;
How like the ghost of what he late appear'd
A' moves before you.
Cal. Shall I answer here,
    Or lend my eare too grossely f *Pen.*
First, his heart 85
    Shall fall in cynders, scorch'd by
your dis- daine,
    E're he will dare, poore man, to ope
an eye On these divine lookes, but with
low-bent thoughts
    Accustng such presumption; as for
words,
A' dares not utter any but of service: 90
    Yet this lost creature loves 'ee. — Be
a princesse
In sweetnesse as in blood; give him his
doome,
Or raise him up to comfort.
Cal. What new change
    Appeares in my behaviour, that thou
dar'st
Tempt my displeasure?
Pen. I must leave the world 95
    To revell in Elizium, and 'tis just
To wish my brother some advantage
here;
Yet, by my best hopes, Ithocles is igno-
rant
Of this pursuit. But if you please to kill
him,
Lend him one angry looke or one harsh
word, 100
And you shall soone conclude how
strong a
power
    Your absolute authority holds over
His life and end.
Cal. You have forgot, Penthea,
    How still I have a father.
Pen. But remember
I am a sister, though to me this brother
105
    Hath beene, you know, unkinde, O,
most un-kinde!
Cal. Christalla, Philema, where are 'ee?
—
Lady,
Your checke lyes in my silence.
96 *in.* Supplied in G-D *Re-" enter*
Christalla and Philema. Both. Madam,
here.
Cal. I thinke 'ee sleepe, 'ee drones; wait

on
Penthea
Unto her lodging. — *Aside."* Ithocles?
wrong'd
lady!
Pen. My reckonings are made even;
death or
fate
    Can now nor strike too soone nor
force too late.
Exeunt. no ACTUS QUARTUS, SCAENA
PRIMA
Ithodes apartment in the palace.
Enter Ithocles and Armostes.
Ithodes. Forbeare your inquisition: cu-
riosity
Is of too subtill and too searching na-
ture,
In feares of love too quicke, too slow of
credit:
I am not what you doubt me.
Armostes. Nephew, be, then,
As I would wish; — all is not right, —
good heaven 5
    Confirme your resolutions for depen-
dance
On worthy ends which may advance
your quiet!
Itho. I did the noble Orgilus much inju-
ry,
But griev'd Penthea more: I now repent
it;
Now, uncle, now; this " now" is now too
late: 10
So provident is folly in sad issue,
That after-wit, like bankrupts debts,
stand tallyed
Without all possibilities of payment.
Sure he's an honest, very honest gentle-
man;
A man of single meaning.
Arm. I beleeve it: 15
    Yet, nephew, 'tis the tongue informes
our eares;
Our eyes can never pierce into the
thoughts,
    For they are lodg'd too inward: —
but I question
No truth in Orgilus. — The princesse,
sir!
Itho. The Princesse? ha!
Arm, With her, the Prince of Argos. »o
Enter Nearchus leading Calantha,
Amelus, Christalla, Philema.
Nearchus. Great faire one, grace my

hopes
with any instance
   Of livery, from the allowance of your favour;
This little sparke.—
Attempts to take a ring from her finger.
Calantha. A toy!
Near. Love feasts on toyes,
   For Cupid is a child — vouchsafe this bounty:
It cannot be deny'd.
Cat. You shall not value, »
   Sweet cozen, at a price what I count cheape;
So cheape, that let him take it who dares stoope
for't,
   And give it at next meeting to a mistresse:
Shee'le thanke him for't, perhaps.
Casts it to Ithocles. Amelus. The ring, sir, is
   The princesses; I could have took it up. *Itho.* Learne manners, prethe. — To the blessed owner, Upon my knees —
25 *In dcnfd Q, beny'd.*
Near. Y'are sawcy. *Cal.* This is pretty!
I am, belike, a mistresse,— wondrous pretty! — Let the man keepe his fortune, since he found it; He's worthy on't.— On, cozen!
It ho. Follow, spaniell; 35
I'le force 'ee to a fawning else.
Amel. You dare not. *Exeunt. Manent Itho. £jf Armost. Arm.* My lord, you were too forward. *Itho.* Looke 'ee, uncle:
Some such there are whose liberall contents
Swarme without care in every sort of plenty;
Who, after full repasts, can lay them downe 40
To sleepe; and they sleepe, uncle: in which
silence
   Their very dreames present 'em choyce of pleasures,
   Pleasures—observe me, uncle—of rare object:
Here heaps of gold, there increments of honors;
Now change of garments, then the votes of
people; 45

Anon varieties of beauties, courting,
In flatteries of the night, exchange of dalliance.
Yet these are still but dreames: give me felicity
Of which my senses waking are partakers,
A reall, visible, materiall happinesse; 50
And then, too, when I stagger in expectance
Of the least comfort that can cherish life:—
I saw it, sir, I saw it; for it came
From her owne hand.
Arm. The princesse threw it t'ee.
Itho. True, and she said — well I remember what. 55
Her cozen prince would beg it.
Arm. Yes, and parted
In anger at your taking on't.
Itho. Penthea!
Oh, thou hast pleaded with a powerfull language!
I want a fee to gratifie thy myrit,
But I will doe —
Arm. What is't you say?
Itho. In anger, 60
In anger let him part; for could his breath,
Like whirlewinds, tosse such servile slaves as
licke
   The dust his footsteps print into a vapour,
It durst not stirre a haire of mine, it should not;
I'de rend it up by th' roots first. To be any
thing 65
   Calantha smiles on, is to be a blessing
More sacred than a petty — Prince of Argos
Can wish to equall or in worth or title.
Arm. Containe your selfe, my lord: Ixion,
ayming
   To embrace Juno, bosom'd but a cloud, 70
   And begat Centaures: 'tis an useful morall:
Ambition hatch'd in clouds of meere opinion
Proves but in birth a prodigie.
Itho. I thanke 'ee;
   Yet, with your licence, I should

seeme uncharitable
   To gentler fate, if rellishing the dainties 75
   Of a soules setled peace, I were so feeble
Not to digest it.
Arm. He deserves small trust
   Who is not privy counsellor to himselfe.
Re-enter Nearcbus, Orgilus, and Amelus.
Near. Brave me?
Org. Your excellence mistakes his temper;
For Ithocles in fashion of his mind 80
   Is beautifull, soft, gentle, the cleare mirror
Of absolute perfection.
Amel. Was't your modesty
   Term'd any of the prince his servants " spaniell"?
Your nurse sure taught you other language.
Itho. Language!
Near. A gallant man at armes is here, a doctor 85 In feats of chivalry, blunt and rough spoken, Vouchsafing not the fustian of civility, Which less rash spirits stile good manners. 88 *leu.* Supplied by G. *Itho.* Manners! *Org.* No more, illustrious sir; 'tis matchlesse
Ithocles.
Near. You might have understood who I am.
Itho. Yes, 90
I did; else — but the presence calm'd th affront;
Y'are cozen to the princesse.
Near. To the king too;
   A certaine instrument that lent supportance
To your collossicke greatnesse—to that king too,
You might have added.
Itho. There is more divinity 95
   In beauty then in majesty.
Arm. O fie, fie! *Near.* This odde youths pride turnes hereticke in loyalty. Sirrah! low mushroms never rivall cedars. *Exeunt Nearchus & Amelus. Itho.* Come backe! What pittifull dull thing am I
So to be tamely scoulded at? Come backe! 100
Let him come backe, and eccho once againe

That scornefull sound of mushrome! Painted

colts, Like heralds coats, guilt o're with crownes and scepters, May bait a muzled lion. *Arm.* Cozen, cozen,

Thy tongue is not thy friend.

Org. In point of honour 105 Discretion knowes no bounds. Amelus told me 'Twas all about a little ring.

Itho. A ring The princesse threw away, and I tooke up:

Admit she threw't to me, what arme of brasse

Can snatch it hence? No; could a' grind the

hoope no

To powder, a' might sooner reach my heart

Then steale and weare one dust on't. — Orgilus,

I am extreamely wrong'd.

Org. A ladies favour

Is not to be so slighted.

Itho. Slighted! *Arm.* Quiet These vaine unruly passions, which will render ye 115

Into a madnesse.

Org. Griefes will have their vent. *Enter Tecnicus. Arm.* Welcome; thou com'st in season, reverend man,

To powre the balsome of a supplying patience

Into the festering wound of ill-spent fury.

ll8 *tupf lying.* G-D, supling.

Org. aside". What makes he here? *Tecnicus.* The hurts are yet but mortall,«o Which shortly will prove deadly. To the king,

Armostes, see in safety thou deliver This seal'd up counsaile; bid him with a constancy

Peruse the secrets of the gods. — O Sparta,

0 Lacedemon! double nam'd, but one 15 In fate: when kingdomes reele,— marke well my saw,—

Their heads must needs be giddy. Tell the king

That henceforth he no more must enquire after

My aged head; Apollo wils it so;

I am for Delphos.

Arm. Not without some conference 130

With our great master.

Tecn. Never more to see him; A greater prince commands me. — Idiocles, *When youth is ripe, and age from time doth part,*

The li,uelesse trunke shall wed the broken heart.

Itho. What's this, if understood?

Tecn. List, Orgilus;i35 Remember what I told thee long before, These teares shall be my witnesse.

Arm. 'Las, good man!

120 *hut.* G-D preserves, but suggests that "not" may be the right word. *Teen. Let craft with curtesie a while conferre. Revenge proves its owne executioner.*

Org. Darke sentences are for Apollo's priests; 14 I am not Oedipus. *Tecn.* My howre is come;

Cheare up the king; farewell to all. — O Sparta,

O Lacedemon!. *Exit Teen.*

Arm. If propheticke fire

Have warm'd this old mans bosome, we might construe His words to fatall sense.

Itho. Leave to the powers 145 Above us the effects of their decrees; My burthen lyes within me. Servile feares

Prevent no great effects. — Divine Calantha!

Arm. The gods be still propitious! —

Exeunt; manet Org. Org. Something oddly

The booke-man prated; yet 'a talk'd it weeping: 15 *Let craft with curtesie a while conferre, Revenge proves its owne executioner.* Conne it again; for what? It shall not puzzle me; 'Tis dotage of a withered braine. — Penthea Forbad me not her presence; I may see her, i55 And gaze my fill: why see her then I may; When, if I faint to speake, I must be silent.

Exit Org. SCENA SECUNDA. *A room in Bassana' house.*

Enter Bassanes, Grausis, and Phulas.

Bassanes. Pray, use your recreations; all the service

I will expect is quietnesse amongst 'ee; Take liberty at home, abroad, at all times,

And in your charities appease the gods Whom I with my distractions have of-

fended. 5

Grausis. Faire blessings on thy heart!

Phulas aside. Here's a rare change; My lord, to cure the itch, is surely gelded;

The cuckold in conceit hath cast his homes.

Bass. Betake 'ee to your severall occasions,

And wherein I have heretofore beene faulty, i

Let your constructions mildly passe it over;

Henceforth I'le study reformation, — more

I have not for employment.

Grau. O, sweet man!

Thou art the very hony-combe of honesty.

Phul. The garland of good-will. — Old lady, hold up 15

Thy reverend snout, and trot behind me softly, As it becomes a moile of ancient carriage.

Exeunt; manet Bass, Bass. Beasts, onely capable of sense, enjoy

The benefit of food and ease with thankfulnesse;

Such silly creatures, with a grudging, kicke

not 20

Against the portion nature hath bestow'd;

But men endow'd with reason and the use

Of reason, to distinguish from the chaffe

Of abject scarscity the quintescence,

Soule, and elixar of the earths abundance, »5

The treasures of the sea, the ayre, nay, heaven,

Repining at these glories of creation,

Are verier beasts than beasts; and of those beasts

The worst am I; I, who was made a monarch

Of what a heart could wish for, a chast wife,

Endevour'd what in me lay to pull downe

That temple built for adoration onely,

And level't in the dust of causelesse scandall.

But, to redeeme a sacrilege so impious,

Humility shall powre before the deities 35

I have incenst, a largesse of more patience

Then their displeased altars can require:

No tempests of commotion shall disquiet

The calmes of my composure.

Enter Orgilus.

Orgilus. I have found thee,

Thou patron of more horrors then the bulke 40

Of manhood, hoop'd about with ribs of iron,

Can cramb within thy brest: Penthea, Bassanes,

36 *largesse.* Q, largenesse.

Curst by thy jealousies,— more, by thy dotage,— Is left a prey to words.

Bass, Exercise

Your trials for addition to my pennance; 45

I am resolv'd.

Org. Play not with misery

Past cure: some angry minister of fate hath

Depos'd the empresse of her soule, her reason,

From its most proper throne; but, what's the

miracle

More new, I, I have seene it, and yet live! jo *Bass.* You may delude my senses, not my judgement;

'Tis anchor'd into a firme resolution;

Dalliance of mirth or wit can ne're unfixe it.

Practise yet further.

Org. May thy death of love to her

Damne all thy comforts to a lasting fast 55

From every joy of life! Thou barren rocke,

By thee we have been split in ken of harbour.

Enter Ithocles, Penthea ber baire about her tares,

Philema, Cbristalla.

Ithocles. Sister, looke up; your Ithocles, your

brother,

Speakes t'ee; why doe you weepe? Deere, turne

not from me:

Here is a killing sight; lo, Bassanes,

60
A lamentable object.

Org. Man, dost see't?

Sports are more gamesome; am I yet in merriment?

Why dost not laugh?

Bass. Divine and best of ladies,

Please to forget my out-rage; mercy ever

Cannot but lodge under a root so excellent: 65

I have cast *off* that cruelty of frenzy

Which once appear'd imposture, and then

jugled

To cheat my sleeps of rest.

Org. Was I in earnest?

Pen. Sure, if we were all sirens, we should sing pittifully,

And 'twere a comely musicke, when in parts 70

One sung anothers knell: the turtle sighes

When he hath lost his mate; and yet some say

A' must be dead first: 'tis a fine deceit

To passe away in a dreame! indeed, I've slept

With mine eyes open a great while. No falshood 75

Equals a broken faith; there's not a haire

Sticks on my head but like a leaden plummet

It sinkes me to the grave: I must creepe thither.

The journey is not long.

Itho. But thou, Penthea, 65 *root.* G-D, roof.

67 *imfmturc.* So G-D. Q, Impostors.

Hast many yeeres, I hope, to number yet, go

E're thou canst travell that way.

Bass. Let the sun first

Be wrap'd up in an everlasting darknesse,

Before the light of nature, chiefly form'd

For the whole worlds delight, feele an ecclipse

So universall.

Org. Wisdome, looke 'ee, begins 85

To rave! — art thou mad too, antiquity?

Pen. Since I was first a wife, I might have beene

Mother to many pretty pratling babes;

They would have smil'd when I smil'd, and, for

certaine,

I should have cry'd when they cry'd: — truly,

brother, 90

My father would have pick'd me out a husband,

And then my little ones had beene no bastards;

But 'tis too late for me to marry now,

I am past child-bearing; 'tis not my fault.

Bass. Fall on me, if there be a burning Etna, 95 And bury me in flames! sweats hot as sulphure Boyle through my pores: affliction hath in store No torture like to this.

Org. Behold a patience!

Lay by thy whyning gray dissimulation,

Doe something worth a chronicle; shew justice 100

Upon the author of this mischiefe; dig out

ti am. Q, swan.

The jealousies that hatch'd this thraldome first

With thine owne ponyard: every anticke rapture

Can roare as thine does.

Itbo. Orgilus, forbeare.

Bass. Disturbe him not; it is a talking motton 10; Provided for my torment. What a foole am I To bawdy passion! E're I'le speake a word, I will looke on and burst. *Pen.* I lov'd you once. *Org.* Thou didst, wrong'd creature, in despite of malice; For it I love thee ever. *Pen.* Spare your hand; no

Beleeve me, I'le not hurt it.

Org. Paine my heart to...

Complaine not though I wring it ard: I'le kisse it; O 'tis a fine soft palme: harke in thine eare; Like whom doe I looke, prethe? nay, no whispering. Goodnesse! we had beene happy: too much happinesse 115

Will make folke proud, they say — but that is he; *Points at Ithocles.* 107 *bawdy.* So Q and G. Changed by D in G-D to *bandy.* sn *Paint my heart to. Q* is corrupt here. G-D omits *paine* and reads

My heart too. W, Pain my heart too.
112-121 *Complaine... ttill 'tis he.* *Q* gives this speech to Orgilus. sc«« H. Efte HBroben Jeart 233
And yet he paid for't home; alas, his heart
Is crept into the cabinet of the princesse;
We shall have points and bridelaces. Remember
When we last gather'd roses in the garden no
I found my wits; but truly you lost yours:
That's he, and still 'tis he.
Itho. Poore soule, how idely
Her fancies guide her tongue.
Bass. aside, Keepe in, vexation,
And breake not into clamour.
Org. aside. She has tutor'd me;
Some powerfull inspiration checks my lazi- nesse. — 125
Now let me kisse your hand, griev'd beauty.
Pen. Kisse it.
Alacke, alacke, his lips be wondrous cold;
Deare soule, h'as lost his colour; have 'ee
seene
A straying heart? all crannies, every drop
Of blood is turn'd to an amethist, 130
Which married bachelours hang in their eares.
Org. Peace usher her into Elizium! —
If this be madnesse, madnesse is an oracle. *Exit Org.* *Itho.* Christalla, Philema, when slept my sister, Her ravings are so wild? *Christalla.* Sir, not these ten dayes. 135 *Philema.* We watch by her continually; besides,
We cannot any way pray her to eat.
Bass. Oh — misery of miseries!
Pen. Take comfort;
You may live well, and dye a good old man.
By yea and nay, an oath not to be broken, 140
If you had joyn'd our hands once in the temple,—
'T was since my father dy'd, for had he liv'd
He would have don't,— I must have call'd you
father.
Oh my wrack'd honour, ruin'd by those tyrants,
A cruell brother and a desperate dotage! »45
There is no peace left for a ravish'd wife
Widdow'd by lawlesse marriage; to all memory
Penthea's, poore Penthea's, name is strumpeted:
But since her blood was season'd by the forfeit
Of noble shame with mixtures of pollution, '5
Her blood—'tis just — be henceforth never
heightned
With tast of sustenance! Starve; let that fulnesse
Whose plurisie hath sever'd faith and modesty —
Forgive me: O, I faint!
Arm. Be not so wilfull,
Sweet neece, to worke thine owne destruction.
Itbo. Nature 155
Will call her daughter monster, — what! not eat?
Refuse the onely ordinary meanes
Which are ordain'd for life? Be not, my sister,
A murthresse to thy selfe. — Hear'st thou this,
Bassanes?
Bass. Fo! I am busie: for I have not thoughts 160 Enow to thinke: all shall be well anon. 'Tis rumbling in my head: there is a mastery In art to fatten and keepe smooth the outside, Yes, and to comfort up the vitall spirits Without the helpe of food; fumes or perfumes, 165 Perfumes or fumes. Let her alone; I'le search out The tricke on't. *Pen.* Lead me gently; heavens reward ye: Griefes are sure friends; they leave, without controule, Nor cure nor comforts for a leprous soule. *Exeunt the maids supporting Pentbea.* *Bass.* I grant t'ee; and will put in practice instantly 170
What you shall still admire: 'tis wonderfull,
'Tis super singular, not to be match'd;
Yet when I've don't, I've don't; ye shall
all thanke mee. *Exit Bassanes.*
Arm. The sight is full of terror.
Itho. On my soule
165 *Q* and *G-D* place a comma after *food.*
Lyes such an infinite clogge of massie dul- nesse, 175
As that I have not sense enough to feele it. —
See, uncle, th'angry thing returnes againe;
Shall's welcome him with thunder? We are
haunted,
And must use exorcisme to conjure downe
This spirit of malevolence.
Arm. Mildly, nephew. 180 *Enter Nearcbus and Amelus.*
Nearchus. I come not, sir, to chide your late
disorder,
Admitting that th'inurement to a roughnesse
In souldiers of your yeares and fortunes, chiefly
So lately prosperous, hath not yet shooke off
The custome of the warre in houres of leisure; 185
Nor shall you need excuse, since y' are to
render
Account to that faire excellence, the princesse,
Who in her private gallery expects it
From your owne mouth alone: I am a messenger
But to her pleasure.
Itho. Excellent Nearchus, 190
Be prince still of my services, and conquer
Without the combat of dispute; I honour 'ee.
Near. The king is on a sudden indispos'd,
177 *tk'angry.* So *G-D* *Q,* th' augury.
Physicians are call'd for; 'twere fit, Armostes,
You should be neere him.
Arm. Sir, I kisse your hands. 195 *Exeunt. Manent Nearcbus & Amelus.* *Near.* Amelus, I perceive Calantha's bosome
Is warm'd with other fires then such as can

Take strength from any fuell of the love
I might address to her: young Ithocles,
Or ever I mistake, is lord ascendant oo
   Of her devotions; one, to speake him truly,
In every disposition nobly fashioned.
Amelus. But can your highnesse brooke
to be so rival'd, Considering th' in-
equality of the persons?
Near. I can, Amelus; for affections in-
jur'd 205 By tyrannie or rigour of com-
pulsion, Like tempest-threatned trees
unfirmely rooted, Ne're spring to timely
growth: observe, for instance, Life-
spent Penthea and unhappy Orgilus.
Amel. How does your grace determine'
Near. To be jealouszio
In publike of what privately I'le further;
And though they shall not know, yet
they shall finde it.
Exeunt omnes. SCENA TERTIA. *An apart-
ment in the palace. Enter Hemophil and
Groneas as leading Amyclas, and plac-
ing him in a cbayre, followed by Ar-
mostes Crotolon, and Prophilus. Amy-
clas.* Our daughter is not neere?
Armostes. She is retired, sir,
Into her gallery.
Amy. Where's the prince our cozen?
Prophilus. New walk'd into the grove,
my lord. *Amy,* All leave us
Except Armostes, and you, Crotolon;
We would be private.
Proph. Health unto your Majesty!
Exeunt Propbilus, Hemophil y Groneas.
Amy. What! Tecnicus is gone? *Arm.* He
is, to Delphos;
And to your royall hands presents this
box.
Amy. Unseale it, good Armostes; therein
lyes
The secrets of the oracle; out with it:
Apollo live our patron! Read, Armostes.
*Arm. The plot in which the vine takes
root*
Begins to dry from head to foot;
The stocke soone withering, want of sap
Doth cause to quaile the budding grape:
But from the neighboring elme a dew
Shall drop and feed the plot anew.
Amy. That is the oracle: what exposition
Makes the philosopher? *Arm.* This brief
one onely: *The plot is Sparta, the dry'd
vine the king;*
The quailing grape his daughter; but
the
*thing 10 Of most importance, not to be
reveafd.*
*Is a neere prince, the elme; the rest con-
ceaFd. Tecnicus. Amy.* Enough; al-
though the opening of this riddle
Is but it selfe a riddle, yet we construe 15
   How neere our lab'ring age drawes to
a rest:
But must Calantha quaile too? that
young grape
   Untimely budded! I could mourne for
her;
Her tendernesse hath yet deserv'd no
rigor
So to be crost by fate.
Arm. You misapply, sir,— 30
   With favour let me speake it,— what
Apollo
Hath clouded in hid sense: I here con-
jecture
Her marriage with some neighb'ring
prince, the dew
   Of which befriending elme shall ever
strengthen Your subjects with a
soveraignty of power.
   »7 *too f* So G-D. *Q,* to; no mark of
punctuation.
Crotolon. Besides, most gracious lord,
the pith of oracles
Is to be then digested when th'events
Expound their truth, not brought as-
soone to light
   As utter'd; Truth is child of Time;
and herein
I finde no scruple, rather cause of com-
fort, 40
   With unity of kingdomes.
Amy. May it prove so,
For weale of this deare nation! —
Where is
   Ithocles? —
   Armostes, Crotolon, when this with-
er'd vine
Of my fraile carkasse on the funerall
pile
Is fir'd into its ashes, let that young man
45
   Be hedg'd about still with your cares
and loves;
Much owe I to his worth, much to his
service.—
Let such as wait come in now.
Arm. All attend here!
*Enter Ithocles, Calantba, Prophilus,
Orgilus, Eupbranea, Hemopbil, and
Groneas.*
Calantba. Deare sir! king! father!
Ithocles. O, my royall master!
Amy. Cleave not my heart, sweet twins
of my life's solace, 50
With your fore-judging feares: there is
no phy- sicke So cunningly restorative
to cherish
   The fall of age, or call backe youth
and vigor,
As your consents in duty: I will shake
off
This languishing disease of time, to
quicken 55
Fresh pleasures in these drooping
houres of sad-
nesse.
   Is faire Euphranea married yet to
Prophilus?
Crot. This morning, gracious lord.
Orgilus. This very morning j
   Which, with your highnesse leave,
you may observe too.
Our sister lookes, me thinks, mirthfull
and
sprightly, 60
   As if her chaster fancy could already
Expound the riddle of her gaine in los-
ing
A trifle maids know onely that they
know not.
Pish! prethe, blush not; 'tis but honest
change
Of-fashion in the garment, loose for
streight, 65
And so the modest maid is made a wife:
Shrewd businesse, is't not, sister?
Euphranea. You are pleasant.
Amy. We thanke thee, Orgilus; this
mirth becomes thee:
But wherefore sits the court in such a si-
lence?
A wedding without revels is not seeme-
ly.
Cal. Your late indisposition, sir, forbade
it.
Amy. Be it thy charge, Calantha, to set
forward
The bridall sports, to which I will be
present,—

If not, at least consenting. Mine owne Ithocles, I have done little for thee yet.
Itho. Y'have built me 75
To the full height I stand in.
Cal. Now or never
May I propose a suit?
Amy. Demand, and have it. *Cal.* Pray, sir, give me this young man, and no further
Account him yours then he deserves in all things
To be thought worthy mine; I will esteeme him 80
According to his merit.
Amy. Still th'art my daughter,
Still grow'st upon my heart. Give me thine hand; Calantha take thine owne; in noble actions Thou'lt find him firme and absolute. I would not Have parted with thee, Ithocles, to any 85
But to a mistresse who is all what I am.
Itho. A change, great king, most wisht for, cause the same. *Cal.* Th' art mine. — Have I now kept my word? *Itho.* Divinely. *Org.* Rich fortunes, guard to favour of a princesse, 76 *Now or never.* G-D, aside Now or never! — 89 *Rich. .. princesse.* G-D, Rich fortunes guard, the favour of a princess. *fortunes. Q,* furtuness.
Rocke thee, brave man, in ever crowned plenty; 90 Y' are minion of the time; be thankfull for it. — *Aside.* Ho, here's a swinge in destiny—apparent!
The youth is up on tiptoe, yet may stumble. *Amy.* On to your recreations. — Now convey me
Unto my bed-chamber: none on his forehead 95 Were a distempered looke.
Omnes. The gods preserve 'ee! *Cal. aside to Ith..* Sweet, be not from my sight. *Ith. aslde to Cal..* My whole felicity. *Exeunt carrying out the king; Orgilus stayes Ithocles. Org.* Shall I be bold, my lord?
Itho. Thou canst not, Orgilus;
Call me thine owne, for Prophilus must henceforth
Be all thy sisters; friendship, though it cease not 100
In marriage, yet is oft at lesse command Then when a single freedome can dispose it.
Org. Most right, my most good lord, my most great lord,
My gracious princely lord,-:—I might adde,
royall.
Itho. Royall! a subject royall?
Org. Why not, pray, sir? 105
The soveraignty of kingdomes in their nonage
Stoop'd to desert, not birth; there's as much
merit
In cleARENESSe of affection as in puddle
Of generation: you have conquer'd love Even in the loveliest; if I greatly erre not, no
The sonne of Venus hath bequeathed his quiver
To Ithocles his manage, by whose arrowes
Calantha's brest is open'd.
Itho. Can't be possible?
Org. I was my selfe a peece of suitor once, And forward in preferment too; so forward, 115 That, speaking truth, I may without offence, sir, Presume to whisper that my hopes and, harke 'ee, My certainty of marriage stood assured With as firme footing, by your leave, as any's Now at this very instant — but —
Itho. 'Tis granted: 110
And for a league of privacy betweene us,
Read o're my bosome and pertake a secret;
The princesse is contracted mine.
Org. Still, why not?
I now applaud her wisdome; when your king-dome
Stands seated in your will secure and setled, 1 I dare pronounce you will be a just monarch: Greece must admire and tremble.
Itho. Then the sweetnesse
Of so imparadis'd a comfort, Orgilus! It is to banquet with the gods.
Org. The glory
Of numerous children, potency of nobles, 13
Bent knees, hearts pav'd to tread on!
Itho. With a friendship
So deare, so fast as thine.
Org. I am unfitting
For office, but for service — *Itho.* Wee'll distinguish
Our fortunes meerely in the title; partners
In all respects else but the bed.
Org. The bed! 135
Forefend it Joves owne jealousie, till lastly
We slip downe in the common earth together;
And there our beds are equall, save some monument
To shew this was the king, and this the subject.
List, what sad sounds are these? — extremely
sad ones. 140 *Itho.* Sure from Penthea's lodgings.
Org. Harke! a voyce too. *Soft sad musiche. A song. Oh, no more, no more, too late Sighes are spent; the burning tapers Of a life as chast as fate, Pure as are unwritten papers, 145 Are burnt out: no beat, no light Now remaines; ' tis ever night.*
Love is dead; let lovers eyes,
Lock'd in endlesse dreames, Th extremes of all extremes, 150 Ope no more, for now Love dyes, Now Love dyes, implying
Loves martyrs must be ever, ever dying.
Itho. Oh my misgiving heart!
Org. A horrid stilnesse
Succeeds this deathfull ayre; let's know the reason: 155 Tread softly; there is mystery in mourning.
Exeunt. SCENA QUARTA. *Apartment of Penthea in the palace. Enter Christalla and Philema, bringing in Penthea in a chaire, vaild; two other servants placing two chaires, one on the one side, and the other with an engine on the other. The maids sit downe at her feet mourning; the servants goe out; meet them Ithocles and Orgilus. Servant aside to Orgilus.* 'Tis done; that on her right hand. *Orgilus.* Good: begone. *Exeunt servants. Ithocles.* Soft peace inrich this roome. *Org.* How fares the lady?
Philema. Dead! *Chrhtalla.* Dead!
P£//. Starv'd!
Cr«. Starv'd!
Itho. Me miserable! *Org.* Tell us
How parted she from life?
Phil. She call'd for musicke,
And begg'd some gentle voyce to tune a farewell 5
To life and griefes: Christalla touch'd

the lute;
I wept the funerall song.
Chris. Which scarce was ended,
But her last breath seal'd up these hollow sounds,
" O cruell Ithocles and injur'd Orgilus! "
So downe she drew her vaile, so dy'd.
Itho. So dy'd! 10 *Org.* Up! you are messengers of death; goe from us;
Here's woe enough to court without a prompter.
Away; and, harke ye, till you see us next,
No sillable that she is dead. —Away!
Exeunt Phil, and Chri.
Keepe a smooth brow. —My lord,—
Itho. Mine onely sister! 15
Another is not left me.
Org. Take that chayre;
I'le seat me here in this: betweene us sits
The object of our sorrowes; some few teares
Wee'll part among us; I perhaps can mixe
One lamentable story to prepare 'em. 20
There, there, sit there, my lord.
Itho. Yes, as you please. *Ithocles sits downe, and is catcht in the engine.*
What meanes this treachery? *Org.*
Caught, you are caught,
Young master: 'tis thy throne of coronation,
Thou foole of greatenesse! See, I take this vaile off;
Survey a beauty wither'd by the flames »j
Of an insulting Phaeton, her brother.
Itho. Thou mean'st to kill me basely.
Org. I foreknew
The last act of her life, and train'd thee hither
To sacrifice a tyrant to a turtle.
You dream't of kingdomes, did 'ee? how to bosome 30
The delicacies of a youngling princesse;
How with this nod to grace that subtill courtier,
How with that frowne to make this noble tremble,
And so forth; whiles Penthea's grones and tortures,

Her agonies, her miseries, afflictions, 35
Ne're toucht upon your thought; as for my injuries,
Alas, they were beneath your royall pitty;
Scene IV. *l&ty »0ben tyWXt* 249
But yet they liv'd, thou proud man, to confound thee: Behold thy fate, this steele!
It ho. Strike home! A courage
As keene as thy revenge shall give it welcome: 40 But, prethe, faint not; if the wound close up, Tent it with double force, and search it deeply. Thou look'st that I should whine and beg compassion,
As loath to leave the vainnesse of my glories;
A statelier resolution armes my confidence, 45
.To cozen thee of honour; neither could I,
With equall tryall of unequall fortune,
By hazard of a duell; 'twere a bravery
Too mighty for a slave intending murther:
On to the execution, and inherit 50
A conflict with thy horrors.
Org. By Apollo,
Thou talk'st a goodly language! for requitall,
I will report thee to thy mistresse richly:
And take this peace along; some few short minutes
Determin'd, my resolves shall quickly follow 55
Thy wrathfull ghost; then, if we tug for mastery,
Pentheas sacred eyes shall lend new courage.
Give me thy hand; be healthfull in thy parting
From lost mortality! thus, thus, I free it.
Stabs him. 59 Stabs him. Q, Kilt him.
Itho. Yet, yet, I scorne to shrinke.
Org. Keepe up thy spirit: 60
I will be gentle even in blood; to linger
Paine, which I strive to cure, were to be cruell.
Stabs him again.
Itho. Nimble in vengeance, I forgive thee;
follow

Safety, with best successe. O may it prosper! —
Penthea, by thy side thy brother bleeds; 65
The earnest of his wrongs to thy forc'd faith.
Thoughts of ambition, or delitious banquet
With beauty, youth, and love, together perish
In my last breath, which on the sacred Altar
Of a long look'd for peace — now — moves — to
heaven. o *Moritur.*
Org. Farewell, faire spring of manhood; henceforth welcome
Best expectation of a noble suffrance:
I'le locke the bodies safe, till what must follow
Shall be approv'd. — Sweet twins, shine stars
for ever!
In vaine they build their hopes, whose life is
shame;
No monument lasts but a happy name.
Exit Orgilus, ACTUS QUINTUS: SCAENA PRIMA. *A room in Bassanes house. Enter Bassanes alone. Bassanes.* Athens, to Athens I have sent, the nursery
Of Greece for learning and the fount of knowledge:
For here in Sparta there's not left amongst us One wise man to direct; we're all turn'd madcaps.
'Tis said Apollo is the god of herbs; 5
Then certainly he knowes the vertue of 'em:
To Delphos I have sent to; if there can be
A helpe for nature, we are sure yet.
Enter Orgilus. Orgilus. Honour
Attend thy counsels ever!
Bass. I beseech thee
With all my heart, let me goe from thee quietly; 10
I will not ought to doe with thee, of all men.
The doublers of a hare, or, in a morning,
Salutes from a splay-footed witch, to drop
Three drops of blood at th'nose just and no more,

7 *sent to.* G-D, sent too. 12 *doublcrs.* G-D, doubles.

Croaking of ravens, or the screech of owles, 15
Are not so boading mischiefe as thy crossing
My private meditations: shun me, prethe;
And if I cannot love thee hartily,
I'le love thee as well as I can.
Org. Noble Bassanes,
   Mistake me not.
Bass. Phew! Then we shall be troubled.
20 Thou wert ordain'd my plague, heaven make me thankfull; And give me patience too, heaven, I beseech thee. *Org,*
Accept a league of amity; for henceforth,
I vow by my best Genius, in a sillable,
Never to speake vexation; I will study 15
   Service and friendship with a zealous sorrow
For my past incivility towards 'ee.
Bass. Heydey! good words, good words! I must beleeve 'em, And be a coxcombe for my labor.
Org. Use not
So hard a language; your misdoubt is cause- lesse: 30
   For instance: if you promise to put on
A constancy of patience, such a patience
As chronicle or history ne're mentioned,
As followes not example, but shall stand
   A wonder and a theame for imitation, 35
   The first, the index pointing to a second,
I will acquaint 'ee with an unmatch'd secret
Whose knowledge to your griefes shall set a
period.
Bass. Thou canst not, Orgilus; 'tis in the power
   Of the gods onely; yet, for satisfaction, 40
   Because I note an earnest in thine utterance,
Unforc'd and naturally free, be resolute
The virgin bayes shall not withstand the light-

ning
With a more carelesse danger than my constancy
   The full of thy relation; could it move ' 45
Distraction in a senselesse marble statue,
It should finde me a rocke: I doe expect now
Some truth of unheard moment.
Org. To your patience
   You must adde privacie, as strong in silence
As mysteries lock'd up in Joves owne bosome. 50
Bass. A skull hid in the earth a treble age,
Shall sooner prate.
Org. Lastly, to such direction
   As the severity of a glorious action
Deserves to lead your wisdome and your judge-
ment,
You ought to yeeld obedience.
Bass. With assurance *ss Of* will and thankfulnesse.
Org. With manly courage
Please then to follow me.
Bass. Where e're, I feare not. *Exeunt omnes.* SCAENE 2. *Aroom of Hate in the palace. Lowd musicke. Enter Groneas and Hemophil leading Eupbranea; Christalla and Pbilema leading Propbilus; Nearfbus supporting Calantha; Crotolon, and Amelus. Cease loud musicke; all mate a stand. Calantha.* We misse our servant Ithocles and Orgilus;
On whom attend they?
Crotolon. My sonne, gracious princesse,
   Whisper'd some new device, to which these revels
   Should be but usher; wherein I conceive
Lord Ithocles and he himselfe are actors. 5
Cal. A faire excuse for absence: as for Bassanes,
   Delights to him are troublesome; Armostes
Is with the king?
Crot. He is.
Cal. On to the dance! ii. *Qfyt* JlBroben

Jrart 255
Deare cozen, hand you the bride; the bride- groome must be
   Intrusted to my courtship: be not jealous, 10
   Euphranea; I shall scarcely prove a temptresse.
Fall to our dance.
Musicke. Nearcbus dances with Eupbranea, Propbilus
with Calantha, Cbristalla with Hemopbil, Philema
with Groneas. Dance the Jirst change; during
which, enter Armostes.
Armostes. The king your father's dead.
In Calantha's eare.
Cal. To the other change.
Arm. Is't possible?
Dance againe. Enter Bassanes.
Bassanes whispers Ca/.. O, madam!
Penthea, poore Penthea's starv'd.
Cal. Beshrew thee!
Lead to the next.
Bass. Amazement duls my senses. 5
Dance againe. Enter Orgilus.
Orgilus whispers Cal.. Brave Ithocles is murther'd, murther'd cruelly. *Cal.* How dull this musicke sounds! strike up more sprightly;
Our footings are not active like our heart,
Which treads the nimbler measure.
Org. I am thunder-strooke.
9 *Deare.* G-D omits. *Last change. Cease musicke. Cal.* So, let us breath a while: — hath not this motion ao
Rais'd fresher colour on your cheeks?
Near. Sweet princesse,
A perfect purity of blood enamels
The beauty of your white.
Cal. We all looke cheerfully:
   And, cozen, 'tis, me thinks, a rare presumption
In any who prefers our lawfull pleasures »5
   Before their owne sowre censure, to interrupt
The custome of this ceremony bluntly.
Near, None dares, lady.
Cal. Yes, yes; some hollow voyce deliver'd to me How that the king was dead.
Arm. The king is dead. 30
That fatall newes was mine; for in mine armes

He breath'd his last, and with his crowne be-
queath'd 'ee
Your mothers wedding ring, which here I tender.
Crot. Most strange!
Cal. Peace crown his ashes!
We are queen, then. 35 *Near.* Long live Calantha! Sparta's soveraigne queene!
Omnes. Long live the queene! 21 *yaur.* G-D, our. *Cal.* What whispered Bassanes? *Bass.* That my Penthea, miserable soule, Was starv'd to death. *Cal.* Shee's happy; she hath finish'd
A long and painefull progresse. — A third mur- mure 4»
    Pierc'd mine unwilling eares.
Org. That Ithocles
Was murther'd; rather butcher'd, had not bravery
Of an undaunted spirit, conquering terror,
Proclaim'd his last act triumph over ruine.
Arm. How! murther'd!
Cal. By whose hand? *Org.* By mine; this weapon 45
Was instrument to my revenge: the reasons
Are just and knowne; quit him of these, and
then
    Never liv'd gentleman of greater merit,
Hope, or abiliment to steere a kingdome.
Crot. Fye, Orgilus!
Euphranea. Fye, brother! *Cal.* You have done it. 50 *Bass.* How it was done let him report, the forfeit
Of whose alleagance to our lawes doth covet
Rigour of justice; but that done it is
Mine eyes have beene an evidence of credit
Too sure to be convinc'd. Armostes, rent not 55
    Thine arteries with hearing the bare circumstances
    Of these calamities: thou'st lost a nephew,
A neece, and I a wife: continue man still;
Make me the patterne of digesting evils,
Who can out-live my mighty ones, not

shrinking 60
At such a pressure as would sinke a soule
Into what's most of death, the worst of horrors.
But I have seal'd a covenant with sadnesse,
And enter'd into bonds without condition
To stand these tempests calmely; marke me,
nobles, 65
    I doe not shed a teare, not for Penthea!
Excellent misery!
Cal. We begin our reigne
    With a first act of justice: thy confession,
Unhappy Orgilus, doomes thee a sentence;
But yet thy fathers or thy sisters presence 70
    Shall be excus'd: give, Crotolon, a blessing
To thy lost sonne: Euphranea, take a farewell,
And both be gone.
Crot. to Org.. Confirme thee, noble sorrow,
In worthy resolution.
Euph. Could my teares speake,
    My griefes were sleight.
Org. All goodnesse dwell amongst yee:
75 75 *goodneue. Q,* gooddeuc.
Enjoy my sister, Prophilus; my vengeance
Aym'd never at thy prejudice.
Cal. Now withdraw.
Exeunt Crotolon, Prophilus £jf 105
Euphranea.
Bloody relator of thy staines in blood,
    For that thou hast reported him whose fortunes
    And life by thee are both at once snatch'd from him, 80
    With honourable mention, make thy choyce
Of what death likes thee best; there's all our
bounty.
    But to excuse delayes, let me, deare cozen,
Intreat you and these lords see execution
Instant before 'ee part.

Near. Your will commands us. 85 *Org.*
One suit, just queene, my last; vouchsafe your clemency
    That by no common hand I be divided
From this my humble frailty.
Cal. To their wisdomes
    Who are to be spectators of thine end
I make the reference: those that are dead 90
    Are dead; had they not now dy'd, of necessity
They must have payd the debt they ow'd to
nature
    One time or other. — Use dispatch, my lords;
Wee'll suddenly prepare our coronation.
Exeunt Calantha, Philema, Christalla.
Arm. 'Tis strange these tragedies should never touch on 95
    Her female pitty.
Bass. She has a masculine spirit:
And wherefore should I pule, and, like a girle,
Put finger in the eye? let's be all toughnesse,
Without distinction betwixt sex and sex.
Near. Now, Orgilus, thy choyce.
Org. To bleed to death. 100 *Arm.* The executioner? *Org.* My selfe, no surgeon;
I am well skilFd in letting blood. Bind fast This arme, that so the pipes may from their conduits
    Convey a full streame. Here's a skilfull instrument:
    Onely I am a beggar to some charity 105
    To speed me in this execution
By lending th'other pricke to th'tother arme,
When this is bubling life out.
Bass. I am for 'ee.
    It most concernes my art, my care, my credit;
Quicke, fillet both his armes.
Org. Gramercy, friendship! no
    Such curtesies are reall which flow cheerefully
Without an expectation of requitall.
Reach me a static in this hand. If a pronenesse
Or custome in my nature from my cradle

Had beene inclin'd to fierce and eager bloodshed, 115
A coward guilt, hid in a coward quaking,
Would have betray'd my fame to ignoble flight
And vagabond pursuit of dreadfull safety:
But looke upon my steddinesse, and scorne not
The sicknesse of my fortune, which since Bas-

no *his. Q, this.* 112 *expectation. Q, expection.*

sanes no
     Was husband to Penthea had laine bed-rid:
We trifle time in words: thus I shew cunning
In opening of a veine too full, too lively.
Arm. Desperate courage!
Org. Honourable infamy!
Hemopbil. I tremble at the sight.
Gromas. Would I were loose! 115
Bass, It sparkles like a lusty wine new broacht;
     The vessell must be sound from which it issues.
     Graspehard this other sticke: I'le be as nimble —
But prethe, looke not pale — have at 'ee! stretch
out Thine arme with vigor and unshooke vertue. 130 *Opens the vein.* 117

betrayed my fame. Q omits my. G-D, betray'd me. 114 *Honourable infamy.* So *Q.* G-D gives this speech to Near-chus. 130 *unshooke.* G-D, *usuhalten.*

Good! O, I envy not *a.* rivall fitted
     To conquer in extremities; this pastime
     Appeares majesticall: some high tun'd poem
     Hereafter shall deliver to posterity
     The writers glory and his subjects triumph. 135
     How is't man' droope not yet.
Org. I feele no palsies:
On a paire royall doe I wait in death;
My soveraigne, as his liegeman; on my mistresse,
As a devoted servant; and on Ithocles,
As if no brave, yet no unworthy enemy: 140
     Nor did I use an engine to intrap

His life, out of a slavish feare to combate
Youth, strength, or cunning, but for that I durst
not
     Ingage the goodnesse of a cause on fortune,
By which his name might have out-fac'd my
vengeance. 14$
     Oh, Tecnicus, inspir'd with Phoebus fire!
I call to mind thy augury, 'twas perfect;
Revenge proves its tnvne executioner.
When feeble man is bending to his mother,
The dust 'a was first fram'd on, thus he totters. 150
Bass. Life's fountaine is dry'd up.
Org. So falls the standards
     Of my prerogative in being a creature!
A mist hangs o're mine eyes; the sun's bright
splendor
     Is clouded in an everlasting shadow:
     Welcome thou yce that sit'st about my heart, 155
     No heat can ever thaw thee. *Dyes.*
Near. Speech hath left him.
Bass. A' has shooke hands with time: his funerall urne
Shall be my charge: remove the bloodlesse bodie.
The coronation must require attendance;
That past, my few dayes can be but one mourn-
ing. *Exeunt.* 160 SCENA TERTIA. *A temple. An aliar covered with white; two lights of virgin wax. Musicke of recorders; during wbich enter foure bearing Ithocles on a hea* r *se or in a cbair e, in a rich robe, andacrowne on his head; place him on one side of the altar. After him enter Calantha in a white robe and crown' d; Eupbranea, Phi-lema, Christalla in white; Nearchus, Armostes, Crotolon, Propbilus, Amelus, Bassanes, Hemophil, and Groneas. Calantha goes and kneeles before the aliar, tbe rest stand off, the women kneeling behind. Cease recorders during her devotions. Sof.te musiche. Calantha and the rest rise, do-*

ing obeysance to the aliar. Calantba.
Our orisons are heard; the gods are mercifull. Now tell me, you whose loyalties payes tribute To us your lawfull soveraigne, how unskilfull
     Your duties or obedience is to render
     Subjection to the scepter of a virgin,
     Who have beene ever fortunate in princes
     Of masculine and stirring composition.
     A woman has enough to governe wisely
     Her owne demeanours, passions, and divisions.
     A nation warlike and inur'd to practice
     Of policy and labour cannot brooke
     A feminate authority: we therefore
     Command your counsaile, how you may advise us
     In choosing of a husband whose abilities
Can better guide this kingdome.
Nearchus. Royall lady,
     Your law is in your will.
Armostes. We have seene tokens
Of constancy too lately to mistrust it.
Crotolon. Yet if your highnesse settle on a choice By your owne judgement both allow'd of,
Sparta may grov
To an increasij
Cal.
     That I forecast nor dangers, hopes, or safety.
Give me some corner of the world to weare out »5
The remnant of the minutes I must number,
Where I may heare no sounds but sad complaints
     Of virgins who have lost contracted partners;
Of husbands howling that their wives were ravisht
     By some untimely fate; of friends divided 30
     By churlish opposition; or of fathers Weeping upon their childrens slaughtered carcasses;
     Or daughters groaning ore their fa-

thers hearses;
And I can dwell there, and with these keepe
consort
    As musicall as theirs. What can you looke for 35
From an old, foolish, peevish, doting man
But crasinesse of age?
Cal. Cozen of Argos.
Near. Madam. *Cal.* Were I presently
To choose you for my lord, He open freely
What articles I would propose to treat on 40
    Before our marriage.
Near. Name them, vertuous lady. *Cal.*
I would presume you would retaine the royalty Of Sparta in her owne bounds; then in Argos Armostes might be viceroy; in Messene
Might Crotolon beare sway; and Bassanes — 45 *Bass.* I, queene! alas, what I?
Cal. Be Sparta's marshall:
The multitudes of high imployments could not
But set a peace to private griefes. These gen-
tlemen,
    Groneas and Hemophil, with worthy pensions
Should wait upon your person in your chamber. 50
I would bestow Christalla on Amelus,
Shee'll prove a constant wife; and Philema
Should into Vesta's temple.
Bass. This is a testament!
    It sounds not like conditions on a marriage.
Near. All this should be perform'd. *Cal.*
Lastly, for Prophilus, 55
He should be, cozen, solemnly invested
In all those honors, titles, and prefer-

ments
Which his deare friend and my neglect-ed hus-
band
Too short a time enjoy'd.
Prophilus. I am unworthy
    To live in your remembrance.
Euphranea. Excellent lady! g *Near.*
Madam, what meanes that word, " ne-glected husband"? *Cal.* Forgive me: now I turne to thee, thou shadow
Of my contracted lord! Beare witnesse all,
I put my mother's wedding ring upon
His finger; 'twas my fathers last be-quest. 65
    Thus I new marry him whose wife I am j
Death shall not separate us. O my lords,
I but deceiv'd your eyes with anticke gesture,
When one newes straight came hudling on another
Of death, and death, and death; still I danc'd
forward; 70
    But it strooke home, and here, and in an instant.
Be such meere women, who with shree-ks and
out-cries
    Can vow a present end to all their sor-rowes,
Yet live to vow new pleasures, and out-live
them:
    They are the silent griefes which cut the hart-strings; 75 Let me dye smiling.
Near. 'Tis a truth too ominous. *Cal.* One kisse on these cold lips, my last!
Cracke, cracke!
    Argos now's Sparta's king. Com-mand the voyces
Which wait at th' altar now to sing the song

I fitted for my end.
Near. Sirs, the song! So *A Song* 74 *vow.*
G-D substitutes *court. All. Glories, pleasures, pomps, delights, and ease, Can but please 7£' outward senses, when the mind
Is not untroubled, or by peace refin'd.
1 Croevnes may flourish and decay, g. Beauties shine, but fade away. 2 Touth may revell, yet it must Lye downe in a bed of dust. 3 Earthly honors flow and wast, Time alone doth change and last. 90 All. Sommies mingled with con-tents prepare Rest for care; Love onely reignes in death: though art Can jind no comfort for a broken heart.*
Calantha dies. Arm. Looke to the queene.
Bass. Her heart is broke indeed. 95
O royall maid, would thou hadst mist this part!
    Yet 'twas a brave one: I must weepe to see
Her smile in death.
Arm. Wise Tecnicus! thus said he:
When youth is ripe, and age from time doth part', The livelesse trunke shall wed the broken heart. 100
    'Tis here fulfill'd.
83 *Th'.* Q is defective in printing here.
84 *It not.* G-D, Is or. sc.ra m. Eljc
HBroben *tytm* 269 *Near.* I am your king.
Omnes. Long live
Nearchus, King of Sparta!
Near. Her last will
Shall never be digrest from: wait in or-der
Upon these faithfull lovers as becomes us.
    The counsels of the gods are never knowne, 105
    Till men can call th' effects of them their owne.

9 781230 353081